Sex and Light!

How
to
Google
your
way
to
Godhood

Alan Richardson

About the Author

Alan Richardson is the author of more than fifteen books, including magical biographies of Dion Fortune, Christine Hartley and William G. Gray. He is also an expert on earth mysteries, mythology, Paganism, Celtic lore, and ancient Egypt. Alan does not belong to any occult group or society, does not take pupils, and does not give lectures or any kind of initiation. He insists on holding down a full-time job in the real world like any other mortal. That, after all, is part and parcel of the real magical path. Please visit his website at *alric.pwp.blueyonder.co.uk*

The first edition of this book was called *The Google Tantra*. This was a title which everyone but me hated, and which seemed to condemn it to instant oblivion — although my elderly aunt quite liked it thinking it was something to do with knitted bathing costumes, for some reason. Then as now, the project had no connection with the company known as Google, which is an internet search engine. Google has neither approved nor disapproved of this whole thing although they were made aware of it from the start, and I suspect they are still supremely indifferent as to whether or not I burnt out my brains and got a sore knob on the way to raising the Kundalini and becoming god-like. Still, if it hadn't been for them I wouldn't have found Margaret across cyber-space in the first place, and this book would never have happened.

Library and Archives Canada Cataloguing in Publication

Richardson, Alan, 1951 -
    Sex and Light; how to Google your way to godhood / Alan Richardson

ISBN 978-1-896238-09-8

    1.Kundalini--Humour. 2. Tantrism--Humour. 3. Sex--Humour. I. Title.

BL1238.56.K86R53   2011 294.5'436   C2010-906840-8

Twin Eagles Publishing

Box 2031
Sechelt BC
V0N 3A0

pblakey@telus.net
604 885 7503

www.twineaglespublishing.webs.com

Prelude

The personal stuff, before we get down and dirty among the chakras ...

Listen, I was a weird child. Just ask me Mam.

When others were jotting down train numbers, learning to smoke, or starting to show a bewildering interest in the curves and cavities of the opposite sex, I was collecting details about chakras, auras, astral projection, earth-bound spirits, yoga asanas, clairvoyance, exorcisms, past lives and all of those lurid topics which became lumped under the dreadful word 'occult'. In a completely solitary way that I would never recommend to my own supremely well-balanced kids, I became deeply, practically involved in all of these things. As I got older (and we're talking mid-teens here) I realised that not many people could cope with this, and those who could seemed even weirder than me, so I kept my distance, and kept my mouth shut, and tried to live a normal life on the surface, doing all the usual things involving sex, drugs and, well not rock 'n roll exactly, but some really lively songs by Simon and Garfunkel. God was I bored.

It was a relief in later years when Margaret appeared, evoked from the aether by a combination of my intuition and the wizardry of Google, and tempted over from Brussels to sample occasional conjugal bliss with me in Wiltshire. Not only was she interested in such inner work, she was reasonably stable, entirely continent, and actively wanted to embrace it. And best of all she made my heart do the river-dance inside my chest.

It all came to a head in the weeks before her birthday. We had just made love on the long couch and she lay beneath me cradling me with her legs, her pale flesh glimmering in the candlelight, breathing deeply and apparently wanting nothing more in the world than this wordless joy. As for me, I was rather hoping she was sated, satisfied, or just plain shagged out. Well she seemed shagged out, and she damn well should have been seeing as we had been at it for hours[1], and the long vanilla scented candle was spluttering into its base, and throwing flickering images of my arse onto the back curtains.

So I figured that at such a vulnerable moment I would make a knightly gesture and ask her what boon she craved for her birthday, smugly certain that she would say something like: "Oh I don't know Alan, you great thrusting beast, you . . . Give me whatever you want." I suppose I should have taken fright by the fact that she didn't pause.

"I want the Serpent Power you've babbled about," she said. "I want to awaken the sexual energies of the chakra rooted at the base of my spine and raise my Kundalini and open my Third Eye and see the Gods. I want to expand my consciousness into divine levels and have the knowledge of all the Worlds, and explore those dimensions which overlap with ours. And I want to do this via magick, strong and hard ..."

Somewhat surprised, I shifted the weight from my elbows to my hands, raised myself like a cobra and looked down into those doe-eyes of hers which can express the ultimate in gentility while never missing a trick.

"Oh all right darling. If that's what you want. But I was thinking more in terms of a new microwave ..."

* * * *

1. *More like two minutes, including chat-up, the act itself, and post-coital Kit-Kat - Margaret*

First things first though. I had to see what I was getting myself – us – into. So I made a brief foray onto the Web looking for the preliminary information we would need, using the same Google search engine which had enabled me to track Margaret down and start courting her across cyber-space in the first place. Tapping in the words, "Raising the Kundalini," brought me a mere 1,430 results, but it seemed to me from just a brief scan of the contents that the whole experience hinged on the notion of the Shakti which cropped up in almost all of them. Looking up that single word brought a hefty 494,000 hits. I just had to start there.

In fact I'll bullet the important points:

- Shakti is the tantric title for the Great Goddess made manifest as a sexual consort.
- Shakti is the innermost awakener of man or god.
- Deep down, every woman is a shakti, or can become one if she wants.

Even the most ordinary woman (if there is such a thing) can act as a Shakti toward her partner, and become other than or greater than herself. Although the word is Sanskrit, it's not an exclusively Eastern concept. The Greeks used the term Psyche, the Romans Anima; the Gnostics talked about Sophia, and the Kabbalists referred to the Shekina. But the Shakti seems to predate them all. And necessarily, every Shakti has her Shiva. Every Moon has her Sun. It is the ultimate female principle. The supreme Divinity.

Not that I was going to worship Margaret you understand, birthday or no birthday, no matter how artfully she wrapped her long legs around me, and thrust her knowing Euro-crutch against mine while whispering things in my ear which would have made my toes curl if I hadn't been wearing new shoes with simulated leather uppers that didn't bend an inch, and made every step seem as if I were crossing the Sea of Tranquillity with Neil Armstrong. No worship from me: I made that clear right from the start, though I don't know why she snorted.

But it was apparent from the early findings that the Shakti represents what some have called the Sacred Whore, a concept which is part of a long and holy tradition of sexual worship. A man and woman can, using certain esoteric techniques, stimulate divine energies within each other. At such levels of consciousness an energy known as the Serpent Power — the kundalini — is awakened: the man and woman evolve to a higher level and become Man and Woman, Shiva and Shakti, God and Goddess, Yang and Yin, Earth and Heaven conjoined ... that sort of thing. Although I've never found it easy to take things on trust, there was obviously a billion people out there on the Web (mostly men) who were going to become my advisers in such matters, and I planned to use large numbers of them on a pick 'n' mix basis.

Mind you I must confess right from the start that I hadn't come to the topic completely ignorant. I did know an extraordinary woman once, called Christine Hartley, who told me that in the late 1930s and during World War II, she had been the Shakti to a man called Kim Seymour, and together they brought through — channelled if you like — energies which have helped make us the best of what we are today. I even wrote their biography, using their secret and sacred personal diaries, called Dancers to the Gods, and you can find that through Google too, if you care to look.

So I had always wanted my own Shakti and to have the chance to become at very least, a living sex god. Perhaps that's what every man wants, unconsciously. Women had come and gone in my life so that it had started to curve like a question mark, but none of them had had the remotest desire to light my serpent fires. Yet now I had a willing Shakti in the supple shape of Margaret, who was only too keen for me to become her Shiva, I wasn't sure how to handle her.

I was a bit afraid, to be honest. There are dark rumours of what can go wrong when the Serpent isn't properly aroused: madness, hyperactivity, schizophrenia and a permanent erection, to summarise the best of the options. I briefly wished that I could have impressed, loved, surprised her for her birthday in some other way — such as by secretly learning French, for example, which is her second language after English and before Flemish, Dutch and Russian.

In fact I'd even started taking lessons in French, with this admirable aim in mind, and was already pretty damned hot on the verb Etre, which some feel means 'To Be', though I'm not totally convinced. The Serpent Power didn't really enter this at all. But hey, what am I, a mage or a mouse? If anyone was gonna lure the Kundalini up from that tricksy little muladhara chakra at the base of her lovely spine, and send it shooting out through the sahasrara on the top of her head and give her whole-body orgasms not to mention knowledge of the Gods, then it was gonna be me.

So this is the true story of how Alan and Margaret, using nothing more than the Internet and the Google search-engine, avoided all those gurus and weekend workshops in which all major credit cards are accepted, risking madness, heresy and badly-defrosted foods as they went all out to find and awaken the Kundalini in each other, and tried to become as Gods despite the Anti-Social Behaviour Order that their neighbours took out on them.

Chapter 1

Kundalini, the serpent power or mystic fire; it is called the serpentine or annular power on account of its spiral-like working or progress in the body of the ascetic developing the power in himself. It is an electric fiery occult, or fohatic power, the great pristine force which underlies all organic and inorganic matter.

H.P. Blavatsky

theosophy-nw.org/theosnw/ctg/kr-kz.htm

What is the Kundalini? Well it's the sort of concept I've taken for granted for many years now without really understanding it, like why we sometimes change down a gear in cars when overtaking, or why bicycles don't fall over, or – most ridiculous of all – why and how butterflies evolve from caterpillars. And don't give me any of that guff about chrysalises and the like, because it still doesn't make sense. So here are some bullet points about it, mainly culled from the first site I accessed: *anaharta.com*.

- 'Kundalini' literally means coiling. That is why it is compared to a snake
- The Kundalini is a great reservoir of creative energy
- Raising the Kundalini can bring cosmic consciousness

- Raising the Kundalini can bring serious mental health problems.

Traditionally it is described as a coiled serpent at the base of the spine, and of course this is not meant literally.

I have to confess that despite the mystical pre-occupations of my childhood, and my ability to memorise and collate vast and useless chunks of esoteric information, I've never had any real knowledge of the Kundalini. Now don't get me wrong, I'm not averse to the odd fib; and in the past I've referred to tantric practises and the Serpent Power as if they were as familiar to me as dear old Aunty Winny who wore carrot-sized wodges of cotton wool in her ears. It was only when Margaret grilled me, in that exasperatingly logical way of hers, that I had to confess that I've neither seen it, sensed it, tickled it, or even so much as come close to it. I knew that if I were to get this tantric project off the ground and have a chance of seeing, sensing and tickling those parts of Margaret which might stir the Serpent Power and bring us both to omniscience, I'd have to be more honest than that. In fact, faced with the possibility that she might withdraw her favours until I got it sorted, I think I dashed to the computer, and Googled, at something just over Mach 1.

"Did you just fart?" Margaret asked.

"That was a sonic boom darling. Remember that my Uncle Neville held the World Air Speed Record in the 1950s. It's in the blood." [2]

She turned her lovely head and thoughts back to finishing off the Belgian magazine La Dernière Heure, after making a sort of clucking noise at the back of her throat. I watched her secretly, doting on her cheeky profile, marvelling that even after two years my heart still leapt at the very sight, smell and taste of her.

Using the cut-and-paste facility which has transformed

2. In September 1953 Neville Duke took the world air speed record from the Americans when his all-red Hawker Hunter reached 728 mph over Tangmere, Kent.

the lives of us writerly types after drudgeful years of Tippex, glue and photocopying, I then managed to memorise a segment from that same site, and declaimed it to Margaret as if it came from *moi*, making sure I maintained full eye-contact and non-threatening body-language:

"Margaret cherie," I said, showing off my increasingly easy grasp of the language. "It's more useful to think of kundalini energy as the very foundation of our consciousness, so when kundalini moves through the sushumna and through our chakras our consciousness necessarily changes with it. The concept of Kundalini can also be examined from a strictly psychological perspective. From this perspective Kundalini can be thought of as a rich source of psychic or libidinous energy in our unconscious."

"Pardon?" she said, looking up from her book on Non-violent Communication and sort of squinnying with those gorgeous deep eyes which seemed to look right through me. "Alan sweety, what does that mean in plain English? What's a chakra? What's a sushumna? What do we mean by psychic or libidinous energy?"

I could see her point. I've spent years sniping at magicians, witches, shamans, druids and mediums who have disappeared up their own basal chakras, most of whom I've written off and verbally decried as being tossers. If I wanted to impress this Shakti of mine and become a tantric master, the first Geordie[3] to raise the kundalini, I'd have to get to basics and find a way to describe these most recondite and esoteric of topics in ways that even my blind Aunty Winny could understand. So let me start from scratch …

* * * *

The first concept we have to learn about is that of Tantra. Tap that single word into the Search box and you get 1,950,000 entries in just 0.07 seconds, so there's an awful lot of people out

---

3. Name given to people from the coal mining areas of Northumberland.

there just aching to say something about it, and define it. It's a powerful sounding word — *Tan-tra* — that some say is actually a composite of tapestry, web and enlightenment.

On the other hand, others insist that the word Tantra is derived from two Sanskrit words *tanoti* and *trayati*. *Tanoti* means to expand consciousness, and *trayati* means to liberate consciousness. And to be honest, that sounds more likely to me. Though you might try and combine them both by saying say that Tantra expands and liberates consciousness, making it the fabric of existence. So the early Tantrics were not so much pounding away hammer and tong, as creating patterns of light and energy. We can try and bullet this too. Tantric techniques include:

- Physical postures (asanas)
- Applying pressure to chakras through squeezing or striking (bandhas)
- Sustained ritual coitus (maithuna)
- Hand gestures (mudras)
- Special breathing techniques (pranayama)
- Use of elaborate visualizations, which may be combined with use of mantras
- Secret methods to open the chakras.

These were taken from *mudrashram.com/glossarypage.html* which appeared top of the list after typing "define tantra" into the search box. It also added that: "Tantric practices often work with the unconscious band of the mind. Practitioners of tantric practices commonly embrace a Dionysian, ecstatic approach to spirituality . . ."

But surely the Tantric adepts were not — could not have been — super-beings. They had lives to live, stomachs to fill, bowels to empty and piles like dreadlocks, just like the rest of us. They probably had jobs, some of them. It's an old Eastern saying that the tramp you meet and scorn by the roadside might be the Buddha, so be nice to him. It should as well be said that the person on the next workbench or desk, or selling the *Big*

Issue,[4] might be an adept at lighting inner fires. Mind you, on a realistic note, I'm sure there's not a woman born who hasn't met hundreds of men claiming to be adept at lighting her inner fires, and offering the mantra: *Howsabouta quickie, darlin'?*

There are real doubts as to where and when Tantra began, though most people place its origins in ancient India. Buddhist Tantra, and Taoism are seen as tributaries from this source. However there is certainly an inner, mystical science of sacred sexuality that dates back thousands of years, not only to India and Tibet, but to the Far East, Polynesia, and indigenous cultures all over the world. The Troubadors made songs about it as they strolled amid the Pyrenees, going from one holy heavy-petting session to another; the Templars had their own secrets devoted to its possibilities, and no-one but the bold would get near their sacred whores; the Cherokees seem to have practised their own form of Tantra called *Quadoshka;* and I even know a man who insists that the Tantra actually started in the Quantocks, in dear old Engerland, and spread eastward in the times before Time and Club 18-30 began. In all places and in all epochs, it was a system which sought to achieve cosmic consciousness, and union with Divinity. Try tapping the individual words Tantra or Troubadors or Taoism or Templars into the search engine, follow the links, and you'll never be seen again.

Dr. Deborah Anapol opined that over a thousand years ago Tantra was actually devised by women, who felt the need for a spiritual movement which embraced the body, the earth, and everyday life. They sought to create a movement which honoured women, rather than limiting spirituality to celibate monks. She felt that today's Feminist Spirituality and Sacred Sexuality movements come from much the same place, and added:

> Sacred Sexuality, or Erotic Spirituality... is a part
> of many spiritual traditions around the world.
> In the last couple of decades elements of Tantra

4. A street newspaper published in eight countries; it is written by professional journalists and sold by homeless individuals.

have been blended or fused with elements from Taoism, Native American, African, Christian, Pagan, and Jewish paths as a basis for re-visioning sexuality. Sacred Sexuality, like Tantra, implies an awareness that sex is the inception of life, of all that is. Without the sexual act, none of us would exist — at least not as incarnate bodies. Sacred Sexuality acknowledges that our life force and our sexual energy originate from the same source. It's an expression of awe and wonder that transcends any particular culture.

lovewithoutlimits.com/erotic_spirituality.html

Today, after only a cursory surf of the Web, Tantra is clearly seen in the west as an alternative, self-help, psycho-sexual, New Agey spiritual phenomenon, a means of creating super-studs or holy whores who have better orgasms at well-attended residential workshops, where great care is given to sexual hygiene and everyone starts by signing cast-iron disclaimers that will avoid all future litigation.

Now there ain't nuthin' wrong with that, as such, but I can't imagine it's real Tantra. The real Tantra is surely a doorway to enlightenment. It's surely to do with expansion of consciousness, and the embracing of love. Certain forms of tantric sex in Dzogchen Tibetan Buddhism, for example, advocate seeing all of life and the universe as the unfolding of one grand sex act, a gloriously cosmic fuck. I think if you can begin to view the world this way, then you can find a route to transformation, Kundalini or no. Though more along these lines later.

But I have to confess that at a very early stage of research, before the practical exercises started, I became quite alarmed. The reason I became alarmed is because of what I found in a piece on Sexual Alchemy (*headmap.org*) which gave advice by the sage Wu Hsien who insisted upon at least 5000 strokes before the male orgasm, in the following pattern:

1 deep 3 shallow [81]
1 deep 5 shallow [81]
1 deep 9 shallow [to 5,000]

I think my first reaction to that is the simple sound of *Gulp!* Sitting on my computer chair and thrusting my hips at an appropriate speed I figured that we were talking about 1 hour and 40 minutes of sheer unremitting thrusting and counting. As I shuffled the chair back from the end of the hallway to its place in front of the console, straightening the rugs as I returned, I wondered: Was I up to it? Could I shag and count at the same time? Had I ever in my life counted higher than 150, and only then during a massive game of Hide and Seek when I was 10, and everyone ran off to catch the bus to Newbiggin.

I could handle the expansion of consciousness; I could do the embracing of Lerv. But a tantalising combination of 5,000 deep and shallow strokes? This was my penis we were talking about, not a Crash Test Dummy. Could I cope with pubes permanently impacted into my Mons Veneris like a pan scourer? And what about my bollocks in all this? They weren't like the demolition balls used knock down old buildings: they were made of flesh, blood, and various squidgy organic things I don't even want to think about. How could they survive the relentless impact?

There had to be more to it than just numerical thrusting with attitude

Trouble is, so many of the Tantric texts and teachings seemed to be dead set against having any fun. They were all up for spiritualising sex, and lifting it to the level of a sacrament, but the prospect of actually enjoying it, and reaching orgasm, seemed to make the sexual gurus suck their breath over their teeth in severe disapproval – assuming they had any breath left after their 5,000 thrusts. The writer of that article on Sexual Alchemy observed that within the esoteric teachings of East and West there is the common belief that the retention of semen is essential to maintaining energy levels, sustaining health, increasing motivation and driving on towards serious spiritual advancement. He — it had to be a he — went on to add that from the same 'esoteric point of view' sex is a good idea and a way of generating and sharing esoteric energy, but that ideally it should not lead to orgasm. In fact, he added, orgasms in general are a bad idea.

Well… I'd like to meet the esotericists who expressed this viewpoint. Had they never chewed the carpet? Had they never made small whimpering noises and temporarily lost the use of their limbs when an attractive woman walked past? In fact, had they ever had sex at all with anyone but themselves? I began seriously to doubt that I could ever sell this no-orgasm deal to Margaret, if that was what raising the kundalini required. She always did have the ability for waking the neighbours (I hoped they would put the noise down to foraging whippoorwills, even though these aren't too common in Wiltshire), but she also wanted to use these same energies to awaken herself. As for me, if becoming a Tantric adept meant that I had to forgo my ability to climax, at least I didn't want to forgo, also, my ability to chuckle — or *glousser*, as Margaret would say, amid the mandarin classes of Brussels.

So the simplest search of the Web would tell you that Tantra, in brief, is a system whereby we can use certain sexually-based techniques to expand consciousness. Actually I knew that already, in those areas of my cerebrum which collected and stored all of that redundant stuff from my youth. But as I said, I didn't yet actually **know**. I wanted full-on, in-yer-face and hopefully on-yer-face-and-wriggling, sexual gnosis. Personal experience which goes beyond mere words. To the best of my knowledge no Geordie had ever achieved that, although thousands of us had had tastes of Nirvana when Kevin Keegan managed Newcastle United the first time. But first I had to throw out everything from the surface levels of my intellect and take it step by step, being sure of my ground, heading toward revelation like the Fool in the tarot who blithely balances on the edge of the abyss, faced with the choice of stepping forward to his death, turning back to safety, or somehow learning to fly.

Let me be blunt. Most of the stuff on the Web was just

pure shite. What I wanted to find was something that might seem touched by real gnosis of the writers' own. Something which might give us a solid and warm basis. Was there anything amid the 1,950,000 Google-generated references for the single word 'Tantra' which might appeal to our hearts, minds and libidos?

Actually there was.

Writers and researchers used to talk about a Library Angel. This is something – a force, an intuition, a mechanism of cosmic serendipity – which will send much needed information into your path whenever you go into the library. I believe in it completely. I've seen books almost throw themselves from the shelves at me, each one containing nuggets of pure gold. Some of my most satisfying mystical experiences have been in the small libraries of small towns. So I had to believe that there is also something of a Web Angel, and invoked it right hard to find some congenial entry into the (so-far) sterile realms of Tantra and Kundalini. And lo and behold, there it was…

Now let me say right off that I don't for one moment believe that Swami Nostradamus Virato is his real name, but you have to give him credit for imagination and colour. I shouldn't mock him (and in fact I don't) coz for a long time in my teens, unknown to all but my Letts *Schoolboy Diary*, I adopted the secret and aweful name of Mahananda. Which means Great Joy, or Great Bliss – even though I was a generally miserable sod at the time. But the article **Tantric Sex: A Spiritual Path of Ecstasy** by Swami Nostradamus Virato wasn't bad at all. I couldn't wait to show my Shakti.

* * * *

She was lying on the couch, reading something light by Heidegger, but even in repose she had the air of a getaway car parked outside the bank with the engine running and the doors unlocked.

"Margaret *ma cherie*, here is something that will make you *glousse, oui?*" I said, hoping she would notice that 40% of my vocabulary was now in French. She went into Attentive Mode, sat up and listened. I lowered my voice, and tried to hint at Great Things. Mastering my breathing I read from the Swami's piece:

> The highest possible synthesis between love and meditation, Tantra is also the connection between the third dimension and other planes of existence beyond mere materiality. While not a religious philosophy, Tantra embraces a deep spiritual understanding of life, and an ancient art of living in harmony with existence … In Tantra, sexual energy is used as the ignition for firing the Kundalini force, the body's biological life-energy system, merging it/you with universal energy. Mystics and metaphysicians call this reaching or achieving Godhead, Nirvana, Samadhi, Mooksha or union with Divinity.

"Yes Alan darling, that's what I want. But you know that already. So how do we go about it? And why are the carpets rucked up as if you'd been rolling back and forward on the computer chair? Is your throat sore?"

I smiled enigmatically, and continued.

> On the Tantric path, we learn to use sexual energy in an extended way, not denying the physical (though nothing is really physical), but going further … deeper … higher. We dance with the electromagnetic force field of our partner, and that dance leads to Cosmic oneness. When this energy is matched and balanced correctly through a loving surrender with a partner, the sparks fly. In that moment of sexual embrace and energy exchange, a couple may achieve a Cosmic orgasm, with their essential selves exiting the body. Those who claim to read auras

can often tell if people are Tantrikas. In Tantra
we learn to open ourselves to others, not only on
the physical but on all levels.

hiddenmysteries.org/spirit/ecstacy/tantra.shtml

"So when do we start?" she asked, picking up another
article to browse, about the thesis, synthesis and antithesis of
Hegelian philosophy and giving me a smouldering Look, and
I'd have done anything for her then. Believe me, anything.

"Soon darling, soon ..." I gulped.

Chapter 2

There is a great danger in raising Kundalini in the first place: it may not turn off or the state it produces may become addictive. Having taught upward meditation for decades, I have seen many cases of aborted careers, broken marriages, disassociated psyches and neurological illnesses that I believe were caused by Kundalini.

Puran Bair
heartseva.com

You can't get far in the Tantra without hearing about the Kundalini, which is the whole point of this book. I tapped that word into Google and it came up with 979,000 entries. Mind you, in an act of juvenile competitiveness and infinite ego, I also tapped my own name into the same search engine and it came up with 1,550,000 entries. I then, without mentioning it to her, put Margaret's name into the search box, and it only came up with 4,240. On the other hand, some of those did actually refer to her.

But first, what does 'Kundalini' mean? As I said at the very start, this is a Sanskrit word meaning either 'coiled up' or 'coiling like a snake.' There are other translations, but they all make some allusion or reference to the serpent nature or serpent power. But is it a purely psychological concept along the lines of ego and id? If not, what is it made of? What is its substance?

"Is it like a clit?" asked Margaret helpfully, showing that curious and almost child-like innocence of hers which is so much at contrast with her hard-nosed wisdom.

Which brings us back, via the bench-mark of dear old Aunty Winny, to my determination to simplify things. If we could avoid all the psuedo-science and/or highly technical jargon, then awakening the Kundalini might become accessible to everyone, and not just the demi-gods. If Winny could understand all this stuff about whole-body orgasms, serpent powers, chakras and the like, then anyone could. Not that she was thick, mind! Hoh no. She kept hens and greyhounds. She could play the piano with more than one finger. She was a fierce member of the local Labour Party. My mam was always frightened of her, and mam terrified me. And while I was into this simplification mode, aiming it all at her mind-set, I realised that in every article about the Shakti, reference was made to the concept of *prana*. And the more I read about prana, the more I began to realise that I should have started here ...

Prana is another Sanskrit word which refers to a universal substance. It underlies everything, everywhere. In the air we breath, in deepest space. If we can get ahold of prana, we can touch the energy of the universe. One of the first definitions I stumbled upon was almost incomprehensible, but I'll give it anyway as an example of what I don't want. It said:

> Quite a number of western translators interpret the energetic phenomena as a form of psychic energy, although the western parapsychological understanding of psychic energy, separated from its cultural-hermeneutic matrix, is probably not the same as the yogic understanding. [*Eh?*] Yogic philosophy understands this concept as a maturing energy that expresses the individual's soteriological longings. [*Wot?!*] Viewed in a mythological context it is also sometimes believed to be an aspect of Shakti, the goddess

and consort of Shiva. [*Ah... **Shakti eh?***]
explanation-guide.info/meaning/Kundalini.html

Well, I'm gonna keep that last sentence: "[Prana] is also sometimes believed to be an aspect of Shakti, the goddess and consort of Shiva", because I'm halfway to understanding it, what with Margaret being my Shakti an' all. But I haven't a clue what the preceding meant; I wanted to get to the basic essence of the topic and keep well away from 'cultural-hermeneutic matrices' — whatever they are. Simplifying the search to the words 'define prana' was much more helpful. I can now say that prana is:

- The life force that operates the sensory, motor, and physiological mechanisms of the body. When this current is completely withdrawn, the body dies. Partial withdrawal of the life force from the muscles results in relaxation; greater withdrawal, numbness and anesthesia; profound withdrawal, paralysis and immobility; full withdrawal, death.
  mudrashram.com/glossarypage.html

- The Sanskrit word for 'breath,' prana stands for the life force, a primordial energy, and it is involved in physical, mental and spiritual health and strength.
  wolfmoongrove.com/Wiccan%20info%20pages/glossary.htm

- In the physical body, prana is the vital breath that sustains life and manifests as thought, bodily function, and physical action. In the cosmos, prana is the sum total of all primal energy that manifests as motion, gravitation, magnetism, etc.
  vedanta.org/wiv/glossary/glossary_mr.html

- The vital breath, which sustains life in a physical body; the primal energy or force, of which other physical forces are manifestations.

- The life force or energy which animates material forms. It is also present in breath. Also Chi, Ki or Mana in other belief systems.

  reiki.nu/treatment/healing/dictionary4/dictionary4.html

- Prana is the energy of the Universe.

  naturesbridge.com/glossary.html

There are many more. The Greeks called it *pneuma*, the Polynesians *mana* and in Hebrew it was *ruah*, which means 'breath of life.' Early Victorians referred to the all-pervading *phlogiston*, which ain't too far from the concept of prana, while others preferred the term *aether.*

There was one piece I Googled on the infinite potential of prana that was quite awesome in the matter-of-factness of its summary. As I understood it, the writer was saying that if you can control prana, then you have the potential for controlling the universe. If you know prana, you know everything.

Many think Pranayama is the control of breath. This is far from true. Pranayama means to know and control the Vital energy or Prana. Control of this mighty energy gives us infinite power. If a man can know and control Prana, what power is there not in him? He can control everything from microcosm to macrocosm, the whole universe comes under his control... All principles have a Unitary principle as the base. If that is comprehended, then everything is comprehended. All powers are but manifestations of that Cosmic Energy, Prana. He who has controlled Prana has controlled all the minds in the universe; all the bodies of the universe: for Prana is the base of all manifestation!

mystic-mouse.co.uk/Wisdom_Texts/

Prana is not simply your breath. It is the substance that underlies everything. If you can become a master or mistress of this, using the techniques of pranayama, then your powers can be unlimited. Well, who can resist a notion like that? This is the Holy Grail of the environmentalists: infinite and renewable energy that can be accessed by everyone! No longer do we have to be subject to the covert agendas of the multi-national companies. We just need to learn how to breathe properly.

Look, it's simple: prana is life energy. If a healer projects it into a patient, he effects healing, and it seems to have several major sources: solar prana, air prana and ground prana, but is more prevalent in certain areas than others. Some of these highly energized areas tend to become healing centers.

I can cope with that, and I'm sure Aunty Winny will get there eventually. Although I think it's time to stop flogging that particular joke.

I first heard of prana when I was in my mid-teens, and became obsessed with the books of T. Lobsang Rampa, of Chakpori Monastery, Tibet. I loved these so much that even when I found out he was really Cyril Hoskins from Thames Ditton, Surrey, it didn't cause me more than a few days of complete psycho-motor malfunction. I learned to do various breathing exercises (known as pranayama), visualising the breath as a brilliant light going in and out of alternative nostrils, filling my soul with radiance. I learned how to make the light shoot up my spine and fountain out of the top of my head and down the egg-shaped sides of my aura. That, I was lead to believe, was one way of viewing and using prana.

So where did Lobsang get it from?

Almost certainly Madame Blavatsky. And if you want to know about the kundalini, tantra, prana, shakti, chakras and all the rest of it, then you just have to look at her, even if she did have something shaped like a cucumber wedged in her vagina which stopped her from ever having ordinary sex, much less tantric sex.

Although she was often described as French, Helena Petrovna Blavastky was born in Ekaterinoslav, Russia, in 1831. She died on May 5th 1891 in London, England. Between those dates she lived the sort of life which ultimately affected us all.

The crucial fact of her life was that in 1875 she founded

the Theosophical Society which, in the decades following, became a hugely popular and highly influential organisation. To us today the remnants of the TS as it is called, seems the very bastion of staid respectability, up there with the Fabian Society, Quakers or Humanists. At the time, it seemed dangerous; no-one had seen anything quite like it. Of course the academics and the Church wrote it off as a mere cult, but then a cult can be defined as any movement you disapprove of - and lots of people disapproved of the TS for lots of reasons. If Spiritualism was by and large for the unlearned masses, Theosophy tended to appeal to the middle classes and the bourgeoisie. It seemed to attract the sort of people who now become aromatherapists, or crystal healers — people who want the cachet and prescriptive powers of a medical doctor but who don't have the brains or the balls to do the training. In many cases a bunch of third rate intellectuals who, while speaking very softly and only saying 'nice' things, imagine themselves first rate.

A lot of the early Theosophists clearly had more money than sense, and some of them financed Blavatsky quite handsomely. HPB (as she was invariably called) took the simple and often primitive tenets of the Spiritualist movement which was sweeping the world like the rock bands of a later century, and among the same class of folk, and cranked it up a few notches with the help of some genuinely learned individuals, a couple of rascal-gurus and of course, the Masters. The Masters were, and some say are, beings of absolute wisdom and awesome powers, with an evolutionary interest in helping the rest of us get to their level. Others insist that they are imaginary beings. Tap Blavatsky into the Search box and you'll get around 217,000 results for that single word, and you can find out more yourself.

The best known of these Masters is Koot Hoomi lal Singh, often called Kuthumi. There was also Serapis Bey, and her own personal guru Morya, whom she first met beside the Serpentine in London's Hyde Park, in moonlight, in 1851. Many people since claim to have communicated with them one way or another.

Tough, loud, magnetic, deeply clairvoyant, an adventurer, a teller of tales and devotee of large cigars and strong hashish … Whatever you think of the Masters, it's hard not to like Madame Blavastky. Her stories of those superhuman beings from Tibet, India, Shamballah and Hyde Park are, well, *exciting*. With or without their help, she performed small miracles on a daily basis — or just faked everything, depending on your attitude. They taught her things, those Masters did, even if they were no more than projections from her own drug-inspired unconscious, bringing the mystic wisdom of the Far East into the sitting rooms of the West. To a society conditioned by centuries of Christian myopia, this was revelatory, mind-expanding, life-changing stuff. For the next few decades, people couldn't get enough of it.

"Do you believe in the Masters?" Margaret asked, who once smoked cigars herself, though never dabbled in drugs, doesn't even like strong tea, but was under the table making *bloop bloop* noises after a kilometer or two of strawberry wine.

Well, sometimes I believe, sometimes I don't. There is a picture of HPB surrounded by them at *enlightenedlife.org* and I must say they look pretty iffy to me. That is to say: if only her Masters didn't have to communicate by letter — even if these were wondrously dematerialised into a special cabinet (which, oddly enough, had a hidden door in the back leading

to her bedroom. God knows why). If only they hadn't been so bland and downright boring in many of their pronouncements, or became used as pawns in the later politico-psychic power-struggles within the TS. If only they hadn't committed plagiary in at least one of their letters to HPB, causing cynics to suggest that HPB had written it herself, cribbing from a recent magazine article. If only ... I suppose there's an answer from me somewhere within those three dots.

Even so, I'm certain she did have some extraordinary powers. I knew a man whose father had known her, and swore that wherever she went within his bookshop he heard strange raps and astral bells, and unearthly music. As her co-founder Colonel Olcott once snapped to a critic: "Do you think that I would stand going about with that mad woman if I did not know what lies behind her."

I showed Margaret a picture of HPB.

"She hasn't had it for years" she commented. "Did she do Tantra?"

Well actually no. No she didn't. Y'see all those early Theosophists were of the opinion that sex of any kind was a drawback to real spiritual progress. Sexual impulses all had to be sublimated or transcended. Chastity, chastity, chastity! Mind you, no-one will persuade me that they weren't all tossing themselves silly in the privacy of their rooms, after their pranayamic exercises and holy meditations, desperately afraid that the Master Kuthumi might materialise behind them and watch. Or worse still send them a stern letter about it, dropping out of the air to land at their feet. Perhaps they were still shackled by their erotophobic upbringings, and felt supported by what they understood or misunderstood from the genuine Eastern teachings that they did access. They were all still afraid of sex back in those days, and it was an attitude that carried on into those Western esoteric movements which later devolved from Theosophy. Mind you, the great and beastly Aleister Crowley put a stop to all that nonsense — but more of Him in due course.

So it was from HPB's writings, such as *Isis Unveiled* and the awesome *The Secret Doctrine*, that we get some idea of what might be termed the 'occult constitution' of Man.

If Margaret were to look at my naked body with her earthly eyes she would see a six foot hunk, thirteen stone of pure muscle, moving toward the remote control with the sinuous grace of a panther. She would, I'm sure she would, contact lenses or no! But if she were to use her inner vision she would see rather more than oiled and glistening bare flesh and rippling six-pack: she would see a creature of Light. That's how we all are. The words 'I Sing Body Electric' from Walt Whitman come to mind, whether it's entirely suitable or not.

So imagine that you are enveloped by an egg-shaped body of light. Visualise it being as broad as your outstretched arms, extending above your head and below your feet. This is the aura. We needn't get bogged down with the Sanskrit terms. In fact, visualising the aura is one of the first things you do when you start any kind of inner work. Some people have large auras; others are shrunken into themselves. Some people are disturbing to be around; others exhilarating. This is all to do with sensing their aura. A powerful, disturbing aura doesn't mean there is anything wrong with that person, just that their energies are different to what you are used to.

Closer to the body, extending only a few inches from the flesh, according to vitality, there is the Etheric. This is sometimes thought of as the Health Aura, because the condition of this determines physical well-being. Visualising and energising the etheric body is also a first step toward self-healing. I don't think the outer aura and the etheric are actually separate, just denser aspects of the same thing. Sometimes people talk about having a torn aura, which can happen after extreme stress or trauma, and through which energy drains away. By healing this rent, the person can get back to normal.

It makes sense to me. Type the word aura into the box, click on the Images tab, then press the Search button and you'll quickly get around 400 intriguing and mostly relevant pictures.

As a teenager I desperately wanted to see the aura. I wanted to study the colours which are said to swirl around the ovoid, through which talented psychics could discern the true nature and status of the soul. I wanted someone to tell me what my aura looked like, and I secretly hoped it was golden.

When I was about 15 I did try to make a machine which would enable me to do this. It involved a sort of hamster wheel on which was fastened seven little squares of see-through coloured cellophane, a crude spectrum in fact. I figured that if this were made to spin with the aid of a little electric motor which I bought for 2/6d from Woolworth's and looked through these panes, then I would see the aura clear as day. My Mam asked me what I was doing. I said I was making a fan. She had immediate and grave worries about my sexual orientation, but it was easier not to explain.

Of course it didn't work, and just fell apart after a couple of revolutions, but there ye go, I tried. Many years later when me and Margaret went to a Psychic Fayre in Glastonbury there was a stall selling Aura Photographs by means of a machine which suggested low-grade electrical tortures. But the photographs on display were smudgy, deeply unsatisfying, not at all like I imagined the aura to be, nowhere near like how I visualised it in many exercises. Most of the examples shown made it seem as if the sitters had had astral tea cozies skewed around their heads. We came away deciding to save money and stick with our inner vision. I bought a nice prawn sandwich instead.

But in certain circumstances I could always see the etheric, like cigarette smoke, following the physical outlines exactly. The ideal circumstances were morning assembly at school, when I could unfocus my gaze and stare at the teachers against the dark backdrop of the stage curtains, trying hard not to stare too much at the slim and sexy art teacher, Miss Jean Paul, whom I fancied rotten. If she ever reads this then I hope she'll know it wasn't a psyochopath giving her such spaced-out Charles Manson-type looks from the seething schoolboy depths. And by the way, her etheric was sublime …

"Is this relevant at all, my precious?" asked Margaret, irritated by that teenage crush of mine, and hoping I wouldn't notice her slow but cunning progress toward the chocolate cake which she had vigorously forsworn.

"Yes, my petal, because when we do get down to tantric sex and raising the Kundalini, we have to be able to understand what will happen to our spiritual bodies. This is not mere flesh and blood, y'know! Tantra is more than just a bit of stiff gristle thrusting into an appropriate slot."

If she had long ago scorned being chaste, then I think

she was just a teensy bit chastened by this tart response of mine. She wasn't giving up though. She read the first daft of the foregoing and said: "Look, don't call this *The Google Tantra* because it's all about you, and your journey."

Well excuuuuuse me! Of course it's about me. And Tantra too! You can't write about such a personal experience as trying to raise the Kundalini without being personal, otherwise it becomes just another New Agey Nuthin', up there with *To Ride a Silver Broomstick*, and *The Celestine Prophecies*, and Carlos Castaneda's novels, and all those books finding (non-existent) secret codes in Da Vinci's paintings, and the even more shitey ones about channelling and walk-ins and crystal healing and past lives. You can't write about Tantra, which involved body mind soul and spirit, without equating and relating it with your own bits, and all those things which have toned and tuned the bits. Besides it's my book and I'm having fun, okay?

So ...

We have the human body which is expressed in the dense matter of the material world, but which is energised by prana as much as blood, and which could be seen at psychic levels as an ovoid glob of light. We can match our breathing with our imagination and visualise the prana filling us, brilliant, healing. We can visualise our auras likewise, and make the pranic energies swirl. And if we feel drained, or out of sorts, then we can rejuvenate our energies by such means. In fact, it could be argued that in reality we are this ovoid glob of light, and that the physical body is just an outer expression of inner spiritual essence. But one step at a time here, eh?

Which brings us to the concept of the chakras. You can't study the images of the aura without seeing them studded onto the human figure. In fact, you can't get far at all in studying occult anatomy before you have to learn about what they are, and what they do. And I must admit I tend to groan when I hear that word, though I'm not sure why. So here goes ...

There are seven chakras. They are very easy to visualise, and by directing consciousness toward them, it is possible to energise them. This is a bit like rubbing a hurt part of your body to send blood flowing to it. The chakras seem to be psychic/ spiritual expressions of functions within the body. Some people (well me, actually) link them with the endrocrine glands. Years ago I even did a drawing showing how these equate. The drawing makes it seem as if I know something solid about endrocrine glands, chakras, and their scientific processes. I don't, but here it is anyway:

Mind you, it's probably easier to see how they work by looking at the following chart. It might not make sense at first, but bear with it. All of this will soon become practical.

Sahasrara Chakra	pituitary gland	violet
Ajna Chakra	pineal gland	indigo
Visuddhi Chakra	thyroid/ parathyroid	blue
Anahata Chakra	thymus	green
Man pura Chakra	adrenal glands	yellow
Swadisthana Chakra	pancreas	orange
Muladhara Chakra	testes or ovaries	red

I think the essential thing to accept is that the chakras can be seen as the spiritual expression of the physical endrocine glands. If one of the latter wasn't functioning properly, you would — if you were psychic enough — be able to diagnose it

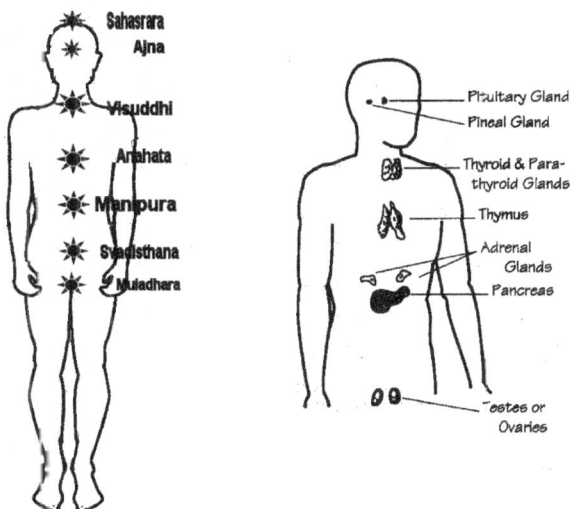

from the corresponding chakra. Just tapping *auric healers* into the box will give you over 8,000 of the buggers. So there are a lot of them out there, although personally I'd try antibiotics first.

It does all seems terribly scientific. The thing is, though, everyone in the West who took on board the early Theosophical teachings became deeply involved in trying to give it all this sort of scientific gloss, which in most cases is no more than psuedo-science. On the other hand, we should probably be aware that 'psuedo-science' can probably be defined in the same way as the word 'cult': as anything that orthodoxy doesn't approve of. In this age of Quantum Physics, all previous scientific dogma is constantly being overturned, and it may be that HPB and the rest were actually more right than wrong in their pronouncements. I've certainly met people who can see the chakras clear as day. I can certainly feel my own ajna chakra swirling like a propellor, when I've tried to agitate it. So I think they do exist.

If we were still to use the traditional scheme, then we have to look at the spine with our inner vision again and see a column of light, the *sushumna*, which connects the base *chakra (muladhara)* with the crown *chakra (sahasrara)*, linking the others en route. Criss-crossing it are two other serpent-like tubes known as the *ida* and *pingala*, which conduct the flow of positive and negative energies, crossing and re-crossing each other up and down the spine.

The image of the caduceus, with the interlinked serpents, is a good version of the ida, pingala and sushumna. The wings at the top represent the explosion of awareness which comes when the initiate has awoken all the centres. Others have pointed out that a more accurate depiction of the ida/pingala/sushumna system can be found in the structure of DNA. But that's another arcanum, and again there are to date 115 images on the Web under the word sushumna alone.

And the point of all this, is that the base of the spine is where the Kundalini is said to dwell. When the Kundalini is aroused it roars up the sushumna, vitalising the chakras in turn with bursts of truly cosmic energy, and explodes out of the top of the head, giving the individual the whole-body orgasm known as horasis, as well as cosmic consciousness.

What can be wrong with that? Well, there are those Terrible Warnings about waking the Kundalini without due preparation and a wise teacher. After all, if the energies are real (and I believe they are), it would be comparable to using electrical equipment when your hands are wet: you might get away with it most times, but there is a very real risk of getting fried.

On the other hand, given the prevailing attitude toward sex generally when the tantric knowledge first came to the West, was this at all similar to all those Victorian warnings about simple masturbation? After all when I first looked up the dread word in a dictionary published in the 1960s, looking all around the library in case anyone was watching, it was still defined as 'bodily self-pollution' — which bewildered me no end, and put me off not one bit. Yet I do believe that there may well be genuine dangers attendant upon waking the Kundalini, and I had to find out what. So, before I dismayed Margaret with even the merest hint of faint-heartedness, I had to answer the question:

Er, *gulp*, listen fellas … what *can* go wrong?

Google found an ominous 13,000 results on the Web for what might be called Kundalini dangers. I didn't think there were so many people out there who had gone so far into this arcane discipline. One of them Kundalini Signs and Symptoms by El Collie even offers a support group *(elcollie.com)* and lists the following symptoms:

- Muscle twitches, cramps or spasms.
- Energy rushes or immense electricity circulating the body
- Itching, vibrating, prickling, tingling, stinging or crawling sensations
- Intense heat or cold
- Involuntary bodily movements (occur more often during meditation, rest or sleep): jerking, tremors, shaking; feeling an inner force pushing one into postures or moving

one's body in unusual ways. (May be misdiagnosed as epilepsy, restless legs syndrome (RLS), or PLMD)
- Alterations in eating and sleeping patterns
- Episodes of extreme hyperactivity or, conversely, overwhelming fatigue (some CFS victims are experiencing Kundalini awakening)
- Intensified or diminished sexual desires
- Headaches, pressures within the skull
- Racing heartbeat, pains in the chest
- Digestive system problems
- Numbness or pain in the limbs (particularly the left foot and leg)
- Pains and blockages anywhere; often in the back and neck (Many cases of FMS are Kundalini-related)
- Emotional outbursts; rapid mood shifts; seemingly unprovoked or excessive episodes of grief, fear, rage, depression
- Spontaneous vocalizations (including laughing and weeping) — are as unintentional and uncontrollable as hiccoughs
- Hearing an inner sound or sounds, classically described as a flute, drum, waterfall, birds singing, bees buzzing but which may also sound like roaring, whooshing, or thunderous noises or like ringing in the ears
- Mental confusion; difficulty concentrating
- Altered states of consciousness: heightened awareness; spontaneous trance states; mystical experiences (if the individual's prior belief system is too threatened by these, they can lead to bouts of psychosis or self-grandiosity)
- Heat, strange activity, and/or blissful sensations in the head, particularly in the crown area.

Well, there are an awful lot of jokes to be made out of that lot, but reading the accompanying letters made me realise that this is all very serious, and that there are some damaged people out there who wouldn't deserve my crassness. On the other hand there were also those who seem to have achieved all that we hoped for, such as:

- Ecstasy, bliss and intervals of tremendous joy, love, peace and compassion
- Psychic experiences: extrasensory perception; out-of-body experiences; past-life memories; astral travel; direct awareness of auras and chakras; contact with spirit guides through inner voices, dreams or visions; healing powers
- Increased creativity: new interests in self-expression and spiritual communication through music, art, poetry, etc.
- Intensified understanding and sensitivity: insight into one's own essence; deeper understanding of spiritual truths; exquisite awareness of one's environment (including 'vibes' from others)
- Enlightenment experiences: direct Knowing of a more expansive reality; transcendent awareness.

"This is serious, you know," said Margaret, looking at me over the top of my own reading glasses, which I bought for £1 from Mick and Sue's Bargain Box, and which she promptly stole. "You either make noises like all the gurus and media-mystics you despise, or you and I really go through with it. Are you afraid?"

Of course I was. And I did know it was serious, and I wasn't playing games. Underneath the banter and the badinage, I really did want to do this. Why? For Margaret's sake? For mine? For the chance of a new type of orgasm? But "suis-je un homme, ou un omelette?" I asked myself, cracking my first French joke.

Oh gosh, I think I'd better explain where I came from, in more ways than one …

Although I live happily in Wiltshire now I came from the North East of England, and was born and raised in a coal-mining town near the coast, called Ashington. Not only is the North the place of darkness, it is also the place where the Dead are said to dwell in many mythologies. So in one sense coming from the North East means rising from the place where death gives way into the life. Ah, go on sneer, but I like that sort of imagery. That old phoney Carl Jung would be proud of me. (Speaking of which, there is even a delightful article by Anthony Daniels entitled Carl Jung: the Madame Blavatsky of Psychotherapy *(newcriterion.com/archive/22/nov03/jung.htm)* which supports my own suspicions about him in that respect.) And if you also wanna look up Ashington on the Web then try *(ashington-ne.co.uk/info/interest.php)* and see all sorts of interesting things that touched me a whole lot more than Jung or Blavatsky ever could. Or you might do the Google Earth thingy and marvel at its endless terraces, and zoom on down to Ariel Street — named after the faery being in The Tempest — where I used to live.

"Alan ... Can you get to the point?" she interjected, looking all soft and lovely in her gold cheong-sam nightie as she browsed through the *Dentists Money Monthly* that a friend of hers had sent, oblivious to the fact that I'd been slaving over a hot mouse for hours.

"Mais certainement, cherie! Is it that you are impatient? Une autre minute, s'il vous plait ..." (Which is French, of course, for gimme a break, darlin'.)

But — and this is the point — I have deep memories of a time between the lives, if you can believe. It was as if I were in a high place, in mist the colour of sperm, looking down at a young-ish couple whom I decided would be my parents. I have no idea what led me to that decision. The man was darker-haired, younger and more vigorous than I ever knew him when he became my Dad; the woman, who wasn't as clearly seen, was more sprightly than the Mam I was to know. 'I' was just a cluster of consciousness. I didn't have any shape. Yet I was aware of deciding that this ageing but still fertile couple, offered the best *possibilities* for me. What I understood by *possibilities* I cannot say. There seemed to be someone else next to me at the time, who had helped me decide.

After that it was simply a case of my spirit falling toward

Matter, as the Gnostics say we do, and being born in Ashington, in the county of Northumberland, England, a place which I can't think of now without feelings which lie somewhere between nostalgia and neuralgia. That was the place I chose, the parents I chose, and the life I chose. Because of this, no-one should indulge in self-pity when their lives don't go as they want, because they are probably going as they themselves, in that space between lives, decided they needed. Likewise, if I'm trying to raise the Kundalini now, it's perhaps because I decided in this spiritual Waiting Room that this was going to be my destiny. Something to do with karma, I suppose.

Hey, but I saw a picture of the Lord of Karma once, in Egyptian mode, as the ibis-headed Thoth. And I must say that when the bills start pouring in, and the jobs go down the tubes, and I'm standing in the sort of bleak and howling places we all know, and nice people keep telling me to look at things from a 'spiritual' viewpoint, I want to meet Thoth between-worlds and take his mask off, look him in the eyes (assuming he's got room for eyes on that pin-sized head of his) and have a right go at him for the bad guidance and adjustments he constantly gives everyone. Don't ever worship the bastards you might meet on the inner planes, no matter how exalted they might appear. And certainly don't trust them.

But listen, there's no denying that I was a weird child. In the first year in the Hirst East Infants School, long before Lobsang's books appeared, I once wandered around the yard reciting the names of the knights who had won the Holy Grail: *Galahad, Perceval* and *Bors, Galahad, Perceval* and *Bors, Galahad, Perceval* and *Bors* ... although I knew that *Bors* didn't get the full experience because he hadn't been chaste — whatever that might mean. And it seemed to me to be grossly unfair that poor Lancelot, the best knight of them all, should have been allowed no more than a glance at the ceremony through the window of the Grail Castle.

It was grossly unfair Lance! You were shafted. None of those virginal prigs were fit to fasten your cuirasses. But maybe I'll deal with the boring Grail and the sad Arthur later when I plan for me and Margaret to deal with — and act out — Western aspects of the tantric tradition. Meanwhile, on reflection, the urge toward Otherness, and magick, and awakening the Kundalini all started after that first time in my life in which I became possessed.[5]

The possession was a wholly benign affair. None of this 360° head turning. This was in the first week after starting infant school, and I had no friends. Mind you, me wandering about in the World War II leather flying helmet that I wore in all weathers to keep the cold wind from my chronically-infected ears, while muttering *Galahad, Perceval and Bors* ... etc. couldn't have helped. So I used to toddle off to the adjoining schoolyard of the Hirst East Secondary School for Girls, where my sister Pat was then Head Girl. *Galahad, Perceval and Bors* ... *Galahad, Perceval and Bors* ...

I was watching them play hockey in the yard when it happened: a sense that I was taken over, that Someone descended into me. It was a consciousness other than my own, but wise and watching, utterly ancient and essentially feminine. It was as if I, little Alan, was pushed to the back of my skull and was allowing this infinitely graceful Being to look out through my eyes and assess how things were going. While this was happening it was as though I was beyond Time and the world: I saw the children in the yard, the big girls playing hockey, and was aware of the noises ... but I was no longer part of it, and watched with complete detachment. Carlos Castaneda uses the term 'Stopping the World' in one of his novels, and that seems to fit what I struggle to explain now. I must have stood there looking blank, and after a few millennia the ball came toward me and our Pat, *Wor Pat* as we would say up there, said *Hello pet!* as she retrieved it. Then the world started again.

It has happened perhaps half a dozen times since, always unexpected, and in each case it was as though *Someone* came down into me to look around and assess, before melting

5. All this will become relevant, I promise, and you will find your own parallels on your own routes toward the Serpent Fire...

away again generally satisfied, leaving me to feel strangely disoriented as the modern and material world clashed back into my perceptions again.

But it meant that by the time I was 14 I knew that I was looking for … *something*. Some book, some insight or experience which might crystallize or explain the inexplicable which rattled inside me. I hadn't discovered girls or masturbation yet and my first love, Lyn Maitland, was still a few years ahead. So a lot of it hinged on that notion the Theosophists used to espouse: 'When the pupil is ready the Master will appear.' The Theosophists used this phrase with simple innocence and elan decades before child molesting became such a problem in society. I was ready enough for enlightenment, but I didn't suppose the Masters were too interested in visiting Ashington, even if the massive and encircling pit heaps did look like the Himalayan mountain fastness of Tibet when they were covered with snow. What I needed was a good book; and I knew the unholy Bible wasn't it. For me, without doubt, it was *You — Forever* by Lobsang Rampa. May his name be blessed!

The book just drew me in when I saw it in the little revolving rack in the newspaper shop on Station Road, next to cowboy novels by Zane Gray and (fourth-best book ever written) *Shane* by Jack Schaeffer. I couldn't have said why I was drawn to that bland title and had never heard of its author before, or the controversy surrounding him. There was nothing on the spine to indicate any supernatural content. There was nothing spicy on the cover to appeal to my exploding libido. Yet it fell open of its own accord and there was a line drawing of a naked young woman and the astral body rising above her, connected by a silver cord, and it felt as though I had been hit by a hammer. I knew this. I had not — then — been out of my body or even heard the term astral projection but I just knew that this was real, and part of what I was looking for, and part of me.

At that moment I realised that I no longer wanted to be an ace fighter-pilot shooting down Russian Migs: I wanted to be a Mystic. I wanted to become like unto a God. Also, as rather a pathetic and wimpish lad I just wanted power, so I could get a bit of revenge – especially against Ron the Neck who was Head of P.E. and who caused me dread, despair and unforgettable humiliations. Well I was no different to any other boy who tried to achieve power via football, sex, trade union politics, marriage or a career, was I?

I had just enough to buy the book. I'm sure my hands quivered as I paid the moustached woman behind the glass counter who bore an unnerving resemblance to the Cisco Kid. I couldn't wait until I got home: I went to the airy and green-painted toilets in the nearby bus-station, sat in a cubicle devouring the contents while, there and then, trying to slip my astral body loose from the surly bonds of the flesh and send my spirit flying up, up! into another realm beyond the pit-heaps, while trying to ignore the graffiti which said in crude letters MAXWELL FUCKS STOATS.

Nothing happened.

Everything happened.

I wrote to Lobsang a few times care of the publishers (taking care to get up early and intercept his replies before the Mam saw and destroyed them) and although his comments were hardly profound, the very fact that this million-copy best-seller had bothered to respond at all was earth-shattering. I had a lucid dream about him once: one day I would write a learned tome called *Literature of the Lama*, and would call myself Mahananda, which means 'Great Bliss.' I read and re-read all his books, and could have recited whole chunks verbatim, as the Tibetan *chelas* had to memorise the holy Kangyur. I even devoured the ones dictated telepathically by his cats.

When I learned the truth about him it didn't really matter because what he said, in such clear and simple terms, touched me, forever. He was my first hero, my first Teacher. And ever since, I've always had a sneaking admiration for cheeky-chappy rascal-gurus like him. But although he claimed to be surrounded by women, I don't think he was getting it any more than Madame Blavatsky, from whom he'd cribbed so many of his ideas. I Googled his name: it got a satisfying 28,700 hits. It doesn't matter how many of them are relevant. This is my hero. There is even a respectful Lobsang Rampa Photo Album at *users.uniserve.com/~dharris/Rampa/Album/photographs. htm* where you can marvel yourself, and I won't have a word said against him. But no, I won't write Literature of the Lama, And I'd rather chew my testicles off and wear spandex than call myself Mahananda these days. Sorry 'bout that, Lobsang.

So you can see, I had no choice. It was meant to be. Margaret, while not having a clue about the Kundalini, had asked me to try and fulfil my childhood dreams, with her involvement. This was not a matter of simple sex tarted up as sacramental sex: it was a destiny! The first Ashington Lad to become a Lord of the Dazzling Face! The first Geordie to become a Time Lord. I wanted the best of things from the check list given earlier. Especially: "Psychic experiences: extrasensory perception; out-of-body experiences; past-life memories; astral travel; direct awareness of auras and chakras; contact with spirit guides through inner voices, dreams or visions; healing powers." All of that lot, hinny, thank ye very much! And after that I wanted to become a Boddhisattva, forgoing nirvana for the sake of all humanity except for Ron the Neck. And it seemed to me then that raising the Kundalini was the best way to achieve all of this. Could I do it? Would I back out? Would I get Thrush?

A poem dropped into my mind, like a sort of nesting bird. It began 'Come to the edge,' though I couldn't remember the rest of it. I thought it was from Milton, but Google quickly brought it up as by the horny little Frenchman Guillaume Appolinaire. There were different translations, but the one I liked best was:

Come to the edge.
"We can't. We are afraid."

Come to the edge.
"We can't. We will fall!"

Come to the edge.
And they came.

And he pushed them.
And they flew.

I wanted to fly, and take Margaret with me. I'd never met anyone like her and wanted to become Yang to her Yin, curling into her warmth at night, and spiralling next to her sense of fun by day. I wouldn't use the hackneyed expression Twin Soul because I've known many wretches say that and in each case their other half has run off with someone else. But there was something deep there, and nothing to do with previous lives. Perhaps the attraction lay in small part because she seemed more faery than human, a sensual, bright, exciting creature of the Sidhe, a kind of Arwen Evenstar but with brains, and I wanted to spend the rest of my life working magick, and chasing serpents, grails and ancient dreams with her.

At that moment however, trying to be brisk and effective, I reminded her of her Kurt Keutzer's comment in **Kundalini FAQ:** "The concept of Kundalini can also be examined from a strictly psychological perspective. From this perspective Kundalini can be thought of as a rich source of psychic or libidinous energy in our unconscious."

"I can go with that," she said, and so could I. "So is there any chance that this is going to work?"

I got my old tarot cards out and asked the pack that very question, and picked the 9 of Cups. It showed a solid, merchant-type sitting in some splendour before a semi-circle of nine large goblets. The meaning given was: 'Concord, contentment, physical bien-etre; also victory, success, advantage; satisfaction for the Querent or person for whom the consultation is made.'

"There you are, petal," I said with some pride. "Shall we Google it now?" The words tarot readings came up with 472,000 results, and I promptly bagged a free one from the site *facade.com/tarot* and asked the same question.

The results were:

Hanged Man (reversed) which represents an important element of the past: Life in suspension. Selfish, materialistic, and untrusting attitudes. Unwillingness to make necessary sacrifices. Going along with the crowd, and refusing to hear the inner voice. Concessions and appeasements that backfire. *(Bollocks – my emphasis.)*

Nine of Pentacles which represents a deciding element of the present. Good luck attending material affairs. Attaining refinement and embracing elegance. Discipline and nobility applied to the maintenance of security and stability. The wise use of resources and foresight. The fulfillment that comes with accomplishment, and the turning of attention to higher things. *(I'll accept that.)*

Three of Cups (reversed) which represents a critical element of the future: A time of shallow overindulgence, followed depletion. The successful but utterly unfulfilling conclusion of a matter. Satisfaction from sensual pleasures divorced from any sense of love. May indicate problems prematurely dismissed or a victory claimed before it is certain. *(Double bollocks.)*

Listen folks, you can — and must challenge the future and challenge it right hard if you don't like the prognostications. Some day I'll write a charming little book about this very notion.

"Can we start now?" Margaret asked, a little wearily and perhaps warily, as I swung away from the PC.

Well, okay …

Chapter 3

Despite cultural differences, actual instructions for what to do during the sex act are remarkably similar from one 'school' of sacred sex to another. This alone is a strong indication that there is a universal biological truth beneath the various forms of tantra and karezza. It is therefore my opinion — and I admit this may be offensive to Hindu and Buddhist tantrikas — that specifically religious instructions can be ignored without damage to the core teaching of tantric sex.

from SACRED SEX by Catherine Yronwode

luckymojo.com/sacredsex.html

We rented a small holiday cottage in St Ives, which gave us a microscopic view of the sea if we bent at obscene angles and peered through the intervening scenery, and if the white horse in the next garden didn't put its stupid, slobbering head in the way. The fire roared in the gas hearth and the candle flames rippled like spirits, giving the evening the possibility of romance, or else an emergency dash for the fire extinguisher.

"Alan, beloved, please please please thrust your enormous and steaming member into me again and again, without mercy, skewering me onto the bed until I scream in ecstasy."

Well, okay, she didn't quite say that. In fact — yes, yes I know — she didn't say anything remotely like that, and she wouldn't like me expressing such a bloke-ishly hopeful False Memory in case her friends in Brussels got the wrong idea of me. What she actually said was: "How shall we start this?" But between you, me, and the other 93 readers, I knew what she really meant, underneath, even if she couldn't bring herself to say it.

I had printed out three different and very simple techniques that we could try on holiday. The first one was, on the surface, very tame, and I didn't even get a stiffy. It came from the web page **The Nights of Antinous** *(liminality.com/ sacredsex.htm)* which, although it was dedicated to the God of Homosexuality, studiously and elegantly avoided tedious gender issues about sacred sex, and showed that the techniques were valid no matter what a person's orientations were, or what hole they wanted to fiddle with. I figured this exercise would be the perfect preliminary. Very gentle and non-threatening. After all, if you want to charm a magick serpent, and make it work for you, then it probably wasn't best to grab it with a pair of pliers. The un-named author wrote:

"Get a partner, and stand or sit facing one another. Look into the other person's eyes; if you're standing, take them by the arms or the hands, and continue looking into their eyes and move slightly, sway from side to side or simply push and pull lightly on each other back and forth. Do not ever break eye contact, do not look away; if your eyes need a rest for a moment, take a 'long blink' of a few seconds, but do not break direct eye contact. Perhaps, begin to synchronize your breathing to this partner's breathing — find a level at which you can mutually maintain fairly deep but conscious breathing, make a compromise to each, try and adopt some of the other's breathing rather than one person completely adapting to the other. Do not consciously try and see into this person's soul or past their eyes, but be open to feeling whatever feelings might come up … Feel the feelings, do what you need to with this — laugh, cry, scowl, move closer or further, move faster or slower — but do not break eye contact. A great deal of sacred sex practice, like the best kinds of partner dancing, should involve constant maintenance of eye contact … Try touching one another in various ways without breaking eye contact; lay your palms on each other's bodies, move them around, explore one another with your fingertips, but maintain eye contact. Do this until it feels right to stop."

"I like the sound of that," she said. And so did I.

There is something very powerful about making eye contact. Some people never can. There is infinite poetry written about eyes being mirrors of the soul, and you'd have to be brain dead, heartless, or incredibly self-absorbed never to have glimpsed searing emotions in a single unguarded flicker of someone's eyes. They can be someone you know well: lover, child, parent; they can be complete strangers you see on the street, and will never see again. Yet you will have been touched, for one blink, by something in their eyes that revealed their inner universe, alive with constellations, lost worlds, Black Holes, and stars going nova.

So we tried that exercise first …

There was nothing particularly ceremonial or sacred about our approach. After supper we lit three small candles, representing past, present and future, turned off the house lights, and Margaret sat astride me (fully clothed) on the couch. Nothing remotely erotic. We tried to synchronise our breathing, as the exercise said, but after the first few huffs and puffs that all went by the board. However we did, both, start to visualise the clear white light of prana suffusing us, filling our lungs and surging out to fill our auras, but she preferred to see it as a turquoise hue, and I went with that.

It was the immediate effect of the eye contact which over-rode all the technical demands of the exercise, though. The willingness to try this made our gazes lock like magnets. For me, the experience was best characterised as Stillness. It verged on another one of those 'stopping the world' moments in which I felt, if not out of Time completely, at least in a part of the river where the greater flow of Time had gone on past, and left me in a backwater touched only by the odd ripple. That sounds very grand, perhaps, but it's as best as I can explain it.

And as our gazes continued to hold I felt an immediate surge of sadness, which I quickly suppressed (don't ask me why), and I watched with wonder as Margaret's face changed: one moment very young, and another very old. Was it the whole sequence of womanhood: Maiden, Mother, Crone? I didn't think that at the time, but I'm inclined to now.

I've no idea how long we did this. We didn't have a clock around, and to measure the exercise in those terms would have defeated the object in any case. But it was probably the sort of ten minutes which felt much, much longer, because as I'm writing this the effect still echoes.

Of course I asked Margaret afterward what she felt, and it took her a little while to find the words.

"Sadness," she offered. "I wanted to cry but felt stupid. I wanted to look away several times but I didn't. I felt a bit exposed. A bit vulnerable. But at the same time I knew that I was very safe."

And that, in essence, was that. Although on the surface this might seem a low-key experience, we both agreed it touched something quite raw. As we carried on the rest of the evening doing the most mundane things, there was still a hint, just a hint, mind you, of this evoked Sorrow inside me. St. Augustine said somewhere that all humans are sad after intercourse, and although I don't go along with that for one moment, and personally vary anywhere between sheer delight and being pathetically grateful, yet I think I know what he was getting at: a sort of Gnostic/Dualist sorrow that we are separate and isolate beings, who can, briefly, glimpse unity and wholeness during lovemaking but have to come back to earth after it. Up like a rocket, down like a stick, as James Joyce would say.

Maybe it was wrong to analyse too much. In essence, we both found emotions within ourselves that we hadn't expected, and as a first step to awakening the Kundalini, we couldn't complain about that.

The next exercise which we tried after a meal at the nearby pub wasn't so much a disaster, as a damp squib. This was again from *headmap.org* on that topic of Sexual Alchemy and wasn't well written (as seen below), although the practical suggestions were intriguing:

> visualising the circulation of energy through your shared connected microcosmic orbits is a further goal during sex
> a common pattern is the figure 8
> tongues and genitals touching, she visualises energy from her sexual center travelling up [inhaling] her central channel crossing through the connection of the two tongues to his body and through the channel running down his front [exhaling] to his cock and back into her body and then cycle repeats. he visualises his energy in parallel being drawn up his spine [inhaling] from his sexual center crossing over to his partner through their touching tongues, down the front of her body [exhaling] to her vagina crossing to his cock and then the cycle repeats
> establishing connections
> use of sympathetic magic, fluids
> breath matching
> non-verbal communication
> verbal communication can be over emphasised in relationships. People can talk to each other just by being together and working together.
> Sex is an important way to speak to your partner without having to say anything.
> Words can get in the way.

Words can get in the way. Tongues can too.

"Come here," I said in a masterly way, waving the printed directions like a ticket to Heaven then putting them on the bed behind her head so I could read them out as I lay on top of her.

"Why don't you put your glasses on Alan?" she suggested after a little while when she realised that the words were doing fuzzy things. "And don't blame Epson this time."

Well we did our best, but every time I tried to visualise the energy passing from my tongue through hers, and then down the front of her body, I tended to end up snorting into her mouth, like a horse. Try as I might, I couldn't get any stallion imagery or comparisons out of this one. I wasn't convinced that the sexual alchemist who wrote this had actually tried it, much less mastered it. Mind you, we shouldn't judge a person's spiritual attainment by his prose, although if you ask me any man who doesn't know the proper use of the semi-colon doesn't deserve to achieve godhood.

The third technique was another gentle one. It's aim was to try and cajole the Kundalini up the sushumna, rather than try to suck it up with a stirrup pump or else blast it from below. It was by Dale Goodyear and boldly entitled **RAISING THE KUNDALINI TO THE LOTUS IN THE HEART.** He describes it as a valuable meditation to help you raise the life and sex energy in the root chakra up to the heart chakra. He adds: "This prevents congestion at the base of the spine and generative organs and releases unwanted and unnecessary pressure there without losing the energy. It lifts up the extra Kundalini to the heart chakra where it can be illumined and refined by the Inner Buddha and used to more quickly attain liberation and enlightenment."

The visualisation is painless. We couldn't wait to try this one together.

> See within your heart chakra the Purple Lotus of Kuan Yin. It has a crystal stem which rises from the base of your spine, drawing your life energy up to that Lotus in the heart center. This is like the action of a flower in a vase of colored

water; the flower draws the water up the stem into itself. You may see your life energy (or kundalini) as violet-purple, as it flows up the crystal stem to the Purple Lotus in the heart center.

The more you practice this, the better it will work. You are creating an upward channel to your heart chakra and then patiently showing your kundalini that it can flow in that upward direction.

How do you show your kundalini? By focusing your attention on the Purple Lotus in the heart center, because wherever you place your attention a magnet is created which draws energy to itself.

groups.msn.com/TRUEBUDDHISM

I confess that I had no clear idea what a lotus actually looks like, so I suggested that we visualise a rose instead, and she agreed. We did this one standing, again by the light of candles, facing each other. We matched our breathing more easily this time, sucking in the prana, seeing the brilliance. Touching her groin and visualising her base chakra I talked her through it, getting her to visualise with me. On an impulse I made the stem of the rose shoot down from her basal chakra and take root in the earth, sending tendrils deep below the soil, down toward the inner earth. As I described this she saw it, and felt it. Then, using my hands as if drawing the energies up, we used the inhalation to make the light rise up the stem as the exercise suggested. As it came to the heart chakra we concentrated on seeing the rosebud open, and the petals receive in all the light of the stars, like a satellite dish. After we held it like this for a while, we reversed the visualisation so that the rose closed up again, and the roots were withdrawn. And then it was my turn, Margaret matching what I had done to her.

This deceptively gentle 'flower' technique was openly

powerful — at least in my experience. It didn't end in the physical region of my heart but carried on of its own volition to open up my whole head. It's hard to describe. As if the narrow cinema-screen of my consciousness was suddenly made almost wrap-around — four times wider and twice as high, if you can assess it like that. I felt light, and swayed physically, as if 'me' was no longer linked to the balance mechanisms of the physical body. As if I were no longer just the flesh, but a sphere of light. It didn't last long because I closed the flower on my own volition, reversing the process again before sitting down and talking about it. To my surprise, however, before I did so I had a kind of brief waking dream of being on the slopes of Solsbury Hill, near Bath, near a small spring. Never having been to the hill, I can't say if this is accurate.

Margaret too had felt the sense of purity, of lightness, and the swaying. She was deeply moved, she looked all melting and lovely and I couldn't help but cuddle her, I felt like a teenager again.

"Was that it?" she asked, as most women seem to ask after they've lost their virginity, and they're reaching for the towel. "Did we raise the Kundalini?"

Non, non, jamais ma petite! When the Kundalini rises, soaring up the sushumna, most people describe it as being like a freight train. Although, when we look at some other sites devoted to offering support or sharing experience, it will become clear that others found it ineffably gentle if done, as they believe, correctly.

She needed a drink. From her loose-limbed manner I reckoned a pint of Sauvignon Blanc would just about do it. Me, I'd settle for a Panda Pop. Honestly, I actually like them. In fact over the years I've lost so much credibility among my native Northumbrians because of this that my vaguely satanic friend Maxwell, once compared me to Walter, Prince of Softies, that character in Beano who is Dennis the Menace's nemesis. And try saying that after a Panda Pop. Actually I tried to do just that, as we got our coats on.

"Will you shut up?" she asked, but in a soft and lovely

way, stepping into the night and closing the door rather firmly after her.

Mind you, I'll confess that I've sometimes wondered if I actually raised the Kundalini years ago, not long after I stopped reading the Beano forever. Or if not raised it properly, at least

tickled it into stirring. I'd read a book on Raja Yoga, and was pretending to be sick so that I could skive school and miss games and the bi-weekly scrotum parade in the showers afterward.

As The Mam stood and did the ironing I lay on the couch pretending to sleep, and put myself into, I fancied, a deep hypnotic trance, breathing steadily, concentrating on the prana going in and out of my nostrils. I lay like this for some time, concentrating as only teenagers can, mindless as the most mindless teenager ever. Then there was a kind of quivering just in front of my coccyx and a light in my head and suddenly my personal space was filled with light — with a brilliant sort of bliss — and I felt an ecstasy without the orgasm, a rippling brilliant power up and down my body, from my arse to my head, surging and pulsing and the very real sense of another person in the room with us. Dark haired and bearded, to me this luminous presence looked like Jesus, yet I could see him without opening my eyes, and he was there, almost rubbing shoulders with The Mam, and I'm just glad she didn't turn coz she couldn't have not seen him. He looked at me with a deeply loving almost amused air, and my heart went out to him. It lasted for seconds; it's still happening yet, as I recall it. There was no noise, just rippling Light, and either an ecstatic peace or a peaceful ecstasy, like a climax of light rather than semen.

That night I put in my Letts *Schoolboy Diary*, with its white plastic cover bearing zodiacal signs, the awesome words: I HAVE SEEN THE LIGHT! but I had to be careful coz I knew The Mam read my diary. (I also had secret symbols for when I wanked, and achieved full astral projection, though not at the same time.)

Immediately after that radiant contact I thought about becoming a Saint as a career option, and spent the evening speaking very softly, like a newly-qualified social worker. But at heart there was no devotional aspect to this. I could accept Jesus as an extraordinary being — a Son of Light perhaps — but as I was well up on Comparative Religion by now I felt that he was just one of many. Son of God? Oh hell no!

I mention this Jesus aspect because there are numerous sites on the Web devoted to Christ and the Kundalini that I don't really want to enter. But the important and measurably memorable part of the experience was this 'rising of the light', this wave-form of bliss which seemed to attract another entity. Was it the Kundalini? Was the being really Jesus? Later, I found out exactly who/what the entity was, but you'll have to wait for that revelation. This is still all relevant. Trust me. It will all loop back upon itself soon, and start to trigger things within yourself that match.

Really, trust me. I'm a helluva holy guru. Honest. And I'll never do weekend workshops, and I don't even have a credit card of my own so I'm hardly likely to ask for yours am I?

One of the first quotes I found when I first dipped into Google was the one given earlier, which I pretended came from my own knowledge: "Certain forms of tantric sex in

Dzogchen Tibetan Buddhism, for example, advocate seeing all of life and the universe as the unfolding of one grand sex act." *(liminalityland.com/ sacredsex.htm)* In truth I do not have the slightest clue about Dzogchen Tibetan Buddhism, but I've always felt that everything which happens, every event, accident and incident, should be seen as a secret dealing between yourself, and the innermost spirit of your Gods. And if your innermost spirit, and your Gods, are necessarily libidinous, then you will naturally see the 'one grand sex act' in the world around.

I was thinking of this when we took the beautiful road from St. Ives to St. Just, and I burbled on about D.H. Lawrence's *The Rainbow.* Although my own dog-eared copy had fallen to bits and by the wayside decades ago, I could still remember the erotic vision that young Bert (from David Herbert Lawrence) had of Nature. I tried to summon it up for Margaret, but it must have seemed as if I were trying to talk dirty, in a meteorological sort of way, so I got her laptop and downloaded the exact quote there and then from: *bibliomania.com*

> They knew the intercourse between heaven and earth, sunshine drawn into the breast and bowels, the rain sucked up in the daytime, nakedness that comes under the wind in autumn, showing the birds' nests no longer worth hiding. Their life and interrelations were such; feeling the pulse and body of the soil, that opened to their furrow for the grain, and became smooth and supple after their ploughing, and clung to their feet with a weight that pulled like desire, lying hard and unresponsive when the crops were to be shorn away. The young corn waved and was silken, and the lustre slid along the limbs of the men who saw it. They took the udder of the cows, the cows yielded milk and pulse against the hands of the men, the pulse of the blood of the teats of the cows beat into the pulse of the hands of the men. They mounted their horses,

and held life between the grip of their knees,
they harnessed their horses at the wagon, and,
with hand on the bridle-rings, drew the heaving
of the horses after their will.

She drove on as I read it out, trying to give it Bert's
Nottinghamshire accent, but I don't think it meant as much to
her. That is tremendously erotic prose, and who could deny its
spirituality? I was inspired. We should have stopped and had
sex in the open fields, in some valley thick with corn, under a
gibbous moon, but she made it clear without actually speaking
that it was no good trying to pull her udder just then, or try to
grip her with my knees. In fact it was March, and so bloody cold
that our thoughts turned more naturally to thicker socks, hats,
vests, scarves, central heating at full blast and double glazing.
Yet I had a marked sense of Bert in my head, or around me,
rather like that time on the couch when the Bearded One had
appeared. Had that last exercise with the flower opened up the
psychic faculties?

It didn't last long, however, and the contact wasn't as
intense, and went entirely when we stopped the car near Zennor
and I got out to look over the landscape. He and his wife Frieda
(nee von Richtofen) had lived near this place during the Great
War, and she had once been arrested on suspicion of signalling
to German submarines, when she had done no more than wave

her scarf and dance in a sort of dervish ecstasy for the wonder
of the day. In their own ways, they were both into Tantra, and
maybe we'll look more at Lawrence's ideas on the topic later.

"I'm not pretending to be Frieda," said Margaret,
anticipating me. "I'm not playing those games."

"Not yet my precious one, my little jewel. But later on
when we try the technique where we become God and Goddess,
Shiva and Shakti, and mate accordingly in a cosmic sort of way,
you'll get very close to that sort of thing."

She gave me a look. I think she was happy to become
part of Shakti and Shiva, makers and breakers of Worlds: Dirty
Bertie and Frieda waving her scarf was a non-starter.

Later we tried the Flower Technique again, on Hayle
Beach, which was utterly deserted and truly beautiful, with
the phallic symbol of Virgina Woolf's Godreavy Lighthouse
before us in the distance, glistening caves in the cliffs behind,
and the sound of waves, the waves, engulfing us. Think of all
the sublime prose you've read about empty beaches and pure
blue sea and that's what we had then. Not another person in
sight, no footprints on the golden sand. It was spoiled only by
the fact that it was so windy we had to bend as we walked, like a
primeval foraging pair of zinjanthropus africanus, no longer on
all fours but not quite ready for full and upright humanity. We
put our hoods up and our backs to the wind, and sort of shouted
the instructions at each other, matching with hand movements
and visualisation as we had done the night before. The results
were the same, but more intense in Margaret's case. She felt
an utter sense of purity (helped by the surroundings, no doubt)
but also had the awareness that things were really being done,
were happening inside her, and that this was not just a string
of impassioned words on a pretty beach. This time we left her
flower open, and carried on.

For myself, I didn't want her to return the favour and do
it to me. I think I felt a slight frisson of fear, in case I might get
entranced while the tide was coming in. Although she had once
been a lifeguard and had no worries in that respect, I myself
can't swim and — I insist — am physiologically, biologically

and genealogically incapable of floating, something to do with small bones, body mass and junk DNA, and I don't care how much she poo-poohs this notion. Put me in the Dead Sea and I'll sink, I'm telling you the truth!

"There there there," she said, not at all consoling, and I think she was taking *le piss*. "Let's go home ..."

We were doing all this work with chakras, and visualising the 'occult constitution' in a way that would have made Madame B. right proud, replete with chakras and flowers and fountains of light, and channels and serpents, but in any reasonable Westerner, with a notionally scientific outlook, there is always the underlying question: do these things actually exist? After all, the whole point of this book is to learn by sheer experience and not simply get hooked on mere words. From a personal viewpoint, my aim was to turn a lifetime's theorising into something practical and applicable and real. But could we make something real that never existed in the first place?

Well, I've known psychics who have never seen chakras, although they still tend to proceed as if they do exist. I've known of yogis who insist on different numbers of chakras, ranging from four to as many as twelve and perhaps more. And I've read about those who link the chakras with things other than the endrocrine glands. And beyond all those, and others, I've also heard of psychics who — I have no reason to doubt them — insist they can see them exactly as described in the ancient texts. So is there really any scientific basis for Kundalini and the chakras? More importantly, do I have to believe that all these chakras physically exist?

Uri Geller, no slouch himself when it comes to demonstrating unusual powers, notes in his website:

> These chakras — nerve plexuses, radiate colorful energies called auras and have been described by Eastern spiritual leaders for thousands of years and currently by countless clairvoyants. Recently they have been confirmed by quantitative electronic

experiments conducted by Valerie V. Hunt, Ed.D., professor emeritus at the University of California (Los Angeles). She told me of her research, reported as "Energy Field Studies - Electronic Aura Study" in Project Report: A Study of Structural Integration from Neuromuscular, Energy Field, and Emotional Approaches, concluded that "the relationship between emotional states and auric color should be viewed as facts and not subjective judgments."

urigeller.com

But perhaps the most practical and approachable attitude comes from dear old Kurt Keutzer again, when he comments:

> There is no compelling work to show that the system represents insights into actual human anatomy. But it's important to understand that kundalini and its network of channels and chakras is simply how yogins have chosen to explain their experience and that yogins from many cultures have arrived at similar, though not identical, concepts. The true physical mechanisms underlying these experiences may be very different from those described. Izaak Benthov has proposed a model to explain kundalini in terms of micro-motion in the brain. In this model, experiences are associated with parts of the body, such as the heart, because the part of the brain associated with that part of the body is stimulated by micro-vibrations. His model is treated in 'The Kundalini Experience' by Sannella ... From a practical perspective

> the key thing is our subjective experience
> and that the roadmap of these subjective
> experiences has been mapped out.
>
> *Kundalini FAQ cad.eecs.berkeley.edu*

I was tempted to invite him around for tea.

So, it gets back to the old notion of acting 'as if.' It's a technique the Jesuits used to enable them to link with the spirit of their Christ, visualising the various stages of the Passion 'as if' they were really present. It's a technique that magicians use when they try to channel the energies behind their Gods and Goddesses, acting 'as if' they were the God Horus, for example, to try and make the link, to actually become the God for a short but infinite while. It's also a technique which is responsible for inspiring just about every evolutionary advance and human cock-up since time began, ranging from Exploration: (let me act as if the horizon wasn't the edge of the flat world); through Politics (let me act as if the next country wanted me to invade); Poetry (let me write as if I really did have a chance with her); Science (let me think as if light could bend); and Crimes against Humanity (let me act as if those people were subhuman). On and on.

I'm not knocking the technique by using these immediate and largely negative examples — just showing how potent it can be. And it has to be admitted, that by acting 'as if' these centres were real both Margaret and I had some very effective and rather moving experiences, even with the brief forays we had made up to this point. The chakras might well have no objective existence, but at least by acting 'as if,' they served to concentrate our awareness in specific places on the human body that had deep and obvious associations — the groin, the heart, the brain …

So before we move on, how nearer does this bring us to awakening the Kundalini, and what exactly have we learned so far? I'm tempted to give a flip answer and paraphrase Howard Carter who, on being asked what he saw when first he peered into Tutankahmun's tomb, answered breathlessly: "Wonderful things …" But Carter was a con-man on a very large scale, and he'd been pillaging the tomb for months beforehand, and the opening was no more than a sham. I think Kurt Keuzer can come in, yet again, with another quote from that same web page:

> It's not useful to sit with our consciousness fixed in our head and think of kundalini as a foreign force running up and down our spine. Unfortunately the serpent image may serve to accentuate this alien nature of the image. It's more useful to think of kundalini energy as the very foundation of our consciousness so that when kundalini moves through our bodies our consciousness necessarily changes with it.

If the Kundalini energy is the very basis of our consciousness, then surely directing our minds toward it must, in the merest degree, nudge, tickle or cajole it - perhaps not into full awakening as yet, but maybe into those levels of dreaming sleep which cause rapid eye movements. If we become aware of it, then it can become aware of us. It seems logical to me. And until Margaret speaks for herself, what have I learned so far?

Well, I've learned that by acting 'as if,' it has been possible to have some very real experiences that are somewhat removed from anything 'usual.' I've learned what it is to actually experience prana and chakra, rather than just see them as concepts on the surface levels of my mind. Also, thanks to Margaret, I've developed some insight and regard into the notion of the Shakti. Was I, was either of us, anywhere closer to raising that legendary beast?

Obviously, the best was yet to come …

Chapter 4

Akashic Records. A theosophical term referring to an universal filing system which records every occurring thought, word, and action. The records are impressed on a subtle substance called akasha ... In Hindu mysticism this akasha is thought to be the primary principle of nature from which the other four natural principles, fire, air, earth, and water, are created. These five principles also represent the five senses of the human being.

A.G.H. themystica.com

There's no doubt that things started to happen. Those simple mind expansion exercises we did stayed with me for a long time after we returned from Cornwall. There was an evening when we lay in bed, watching the shadows on the wall from the occasional passing traffic, listening to the ticking clock, and the movements of people in the other apartments, and all was very gentle, and we both knew we'd drift off to sleep before too long. Margaret lay against me, sort of salivating into my armpit as she muttered softly about her simple everyday concerns, chief of which seemed to be the origin of consciousness in the breakdown of the bi-cameral mind and the impact this had had on European psyches, and her voice was like the sound of a calm sea stroking a beach. And as for me ... well, I wasn't quite all there.

Physically I was there, oh yes! Thirteen stone of hard muscle stretched next to her, the old Beano annual she had bought me propped on my manly chest and one armed draped protectively around her silken shoulders. But mentally... I was in a different world.

I think it was Carl Jung who coined the terms hypnagogic and hypnopompic — intensely real images which can float through the mind before sleep or before waking. I couldn't remember which, and vowed to look it up via Google the next day.

Basically it was as though my brow had opened up into a very wide, virtual reality cinema screen, and I was looking into another room. I was not just looking, I was actually standing on the edge of it. The room was empty, and it was a classroom. The windows were high on the wall, presumably to discourage pupils from looking out, and a few desks were pushed to the side as if to make space for something about to start. It had the sense of being in the 1950s, and I felt that it was in Scotland, though there was nothing, no person or clue present, to make me think that. There was no emotion present in the experience, no symbolism that I could discern, nothing obvious from my own childhood which I could equate it with, and it was, not just intensely real, actually real.

"Alan darling," Margaret whispered, and I was fully aware of her, fully aware of everything around even though I wasn't properly engaged with it. "Stop reading about Walter, Prince of Softies ... Where are you?"

So I told her, and the vision didn't break, and I was still aware of the outer world.

And that, basically, was that.

There was a precedent for this, and Madame Blavatsky

provided it. I remembered reading a long time ago about how she wrote her classic tome The Secret Doctrine, and Googled just the paragraph I needed, where it quoted her as saying:

> Well, you see, what I do is this. I make what I can only describe as a sort of vacuum in the air before me, and fix my sight and my will upon it, and soon scene after scene passes before me like the successive pictures of a diorama, or, if I need a reference or information from some book, I fix my mind intently, and the astral counterpart of the book appears, and from it I take what I need. The more perfectly my mind is freed from distractions and mortifications, the more energy and intentness it possesses, the more easily I can do this …
>
> *katinkahesselink.net/index*

I was struck by the parallel between what HPB was doing, and what everyone does these days when they surf the Web. Or rather the converse was true: as I surfed the Web, with my sight fixed on the monitor and the infinite scenes, references and information passing before me, I had a memory of HPB's words and was suddenly struck by the parallel between what we were both doing.

I Googled this too, and it provided a piece from the present-day admirers of the late great seer and prophet Edgar Cayce which agreed with this notion:

> The Akashic Records or "The Book of Life" can be equated to the universe's super computer system. It is this system that acts as the central storehouse of all information for every individual who has ever lived upon the earth. More than

> just a reservoir of events, the Akashic
> Records contain every deed, word,
> feeling, thought, and intent that has
> ever occurred at any time in the history
> of the world. Much more than simply
> a memory storehouse, however, these
> Akashic Records are interactive in that
> they have a tremendous influence upon
> our everyday lives, our relationships,
> our feelings and belief systems, and the
> potential realities we draw toward us.
>
> *edgarcayce.org/about_ec/cayce_on/akashic*

Given that, you can't help but draw comparisons
between the 'Halls of the Akasha' as they are sometimes called,
and the World Wide Web. Lobsang, drawing upon the mad
Russian woman, wrote about how you could access all history
— all of it, past and future history — once you learned to read
the akashic records. The intriguing thing was, he said, you
didn't just see it, you experienced it. If you wanted to know
how William the Bastard got his lucky victory at Hastings, in
1066, you would see it from his eyes, as if in his head, from
his emotional and moral point of view, like the greatest Virtual
Reality experience you could possibly imagine. Some compare
these records to a cosmic or collective consciousness. Following
from this, it is clear that each person's website is an extension
or expression of his or her mind. When we access them, we are
seeing things from their point of view.

Who knows how intimately we may be able to do this
with the computer technologies of the future? Will man and
computer unite? Will the World Wide Web and the Halls of the
Akasha merge? In fact, could we parallel the Gods themselves
with the Internet Service Providers? And do we ever think of the
ISPs as jealous or vindictive (like Jehovah), or yet all-providing
and all merciful - but with a catch? Of course we do! And what
roles in the electric cosmos do Windows and Linux and the rest
of the Operating Systems parallel? And where does Apple-Mac

fit into this cosmology? And are the Search Engines comparable to the Recording Angels? Or is the Google I use one and the same as Thoth in his role as cosmic scribe? If so…

A geeky type could have some fun here, but I didn't want to go too far down this path yet, because my primary aim was still to become a Geordie Sex God by raising the Kundalini. Nevertheless, if that act is said to bring an expansion of consciousness toward divine levels, then just attempting the act seemed to provoke a little burst of, for me, unusual insight.

Of course the Web isn't an exact parallel, but it's not too different. All human life is there, including much I'd rather not know about (especially all the spam I get regarding penis enlargements and cheap oh-so-cheap Viagra dear Mr Alan). But as with the Akashic records, you read and see life from the viewpoint of those around whom the web site functions.

The point is this: Was the benign possession I used to experience an example of someone in the future reading the Akashic records to assess me? Is that incredible arrogance? Or was it just me visiting myself, as I sometimes think? This ain't hard science, but it makes a workable kind of sense, and I intended to act 'as if' in order to get where I wanted to go.

This Web Angel certainly tended to come up with the goods to such an extent that I had come to feel a certain symbiosis with the computer, as if - like Alice - I had been sucked through the screen and was actively involved in the world beyond. While I merely looked for a simple definition of the terms hypnogogic and hypnopompic, I ended up stumbling into, or having thrown up at me, references which were unexpectedly but exquisitely apt, and which showed that I was on the right track even if it felt at times that I was lost.

Simon J. Sherwood in the Department of Psychology at the University of Edinburgh, wrote in *geocities.yahoo.com* that a whole range of anomalous experiences have been reported during the hypnogogic or hypnopompic states which surround periods of sleep. He points out that it is not uncommon for people to experience brief, vivid and often strange imagery or to find themselves temporarily unable to move or speak during these periods between wakefulness and sleep:

> These brief sensations and the temporary
> paralysis are known as 'hypnogogic'
> or 'hypnopompic' imagery and 'sleep
> paralysis,' respectively... More specifically,
> hypnogogic/hypnopompic imagery
> has been associated with reports of
> extrasensory perception (ESP), apparitions
> and communication with the dead, out-
> of-the-body experiences (OBEs), visions
> of past lives and experiences involving
> extraterrestrials ... In addition to the above
> anomalous experiences, sleep paralysis
> has also been associated with reports
> of psychokinesis (PK), and near-death
> experiences (NDEs).

So I was willing to act as if that vision of the empty
room, and perhaps also that glimpse of Solsbury Hill, was
symptomatic of the Kundalini stirring within me, and I just
couldn't wait for the extra-terrestrials to arrive so I could be
the first Englishman to have trans-human sex in Earth orbit.
Although I didn't plan on telling Margaret that.

But seriously, the one thing I will never joke about
are the inner experiences themselves, and I really felt that in
some sense my mind was already opening, and that the dense,
material and ever-so-mundane world was thinning out a bit.

Enough. Let's get down to something practical.

When Margaret came back from Gomorrah, aka Brussels, I
had two pieces already downloaded for her, the first of them
from the colourful site called **Kundalini Shakti** at: *kaalchakra0.
tripod.com/id20.html* and entitled 'Pranayama for Awakening the
Kundalini,' followed by 'Kundalini Pranayama.'

Mind you before we started, before she even had time to
do her anal, no touching, no snogging, furrowed-brow routine

of emptying her suitcases to the very last thong, I was sitting on the end of the bed in a semi-lotus posture, reading out some of the pre-requisites insisted upon by the yogi:

> The student should observe perfect discipline. He must be civil, polite, courteous, gentle, noble and gracious in his behaviour. He must have perseverance, adamantine will, asinine patience and leech-like tenacity... He must be perfectly self-controlled, pure and devoted to the Guru.

That was *moi*, I had all of those qualities!

"No, you've got some of them," she said obliquely, gritting her teeth and muttering in several languages about needing some space to unpack. I made a mental note to check the concept of 'glossolalia' - speaking in tongues - on the internet *asap*.

But who was my Guru? I mused. Was it Google? Was it Internet Explorer or Mozilla Firefox?

"Alan ..." she sighed. Now a lesser man would regard that sigh as a mixture of exasperation and exhaustion after the long drive, but I knew it was sublimated passion. "Just stop burbling would you?"

Well I had to start by myself, there and then, as she sorted out her clothes and spread her knickers on the duvet like tarot cards. I was excited by the statement: "This Pranayama will awaken the Kundalini quickly." Well that's what I wanted! Margaret could do as Margaret would, which at that moment seemed to involve crashing around the room like a rip-tide. The technique itself was attractively simple.

> When you practise the following, concentrate on the Muladhara Chakra at the base of the spinal column, which is triangular in form and which is the seat

of the Kundalini Shakti. Close the right nostril with your right thumb. Inhale through the left nostril till you count 3 Oms slowly. Imagine that you are drawing the Prana with the atmospheric air. Then close the left nostril with your little and ring fingers of the right hand. Then retain the breath for 12 Oms. Send the current down the spinal column straight into the triangular lotus, the Muladhara Chakra. Imagine that the nerve-current is striking against the lotus and awakening the Kundalini. Then slowly exhale through the right nostril counting 6 Oms. Repeat the process from the right nostril as stated above, using the same units, and having the same imagination and feeling.

Like a good doctor, he said that it must be done 3 times in the morning and 3 times in the evening, increasing the number and time gradually and cautiously according to my strength and capacity. As long as I concentrated on the Muladhara Chakra he assured me that the Kundalini would be awakened quickly as long as my concentration was intense and if the pranayama was practised regularly.

Well, call me pigeon-chested if you like, slag me off for a wimpish lung capacity, but the counts of 3 for the inhale, 12 for the retention, and 6 for the exhale just didn't feel natural. I was breathing out more than I was taking in. And how exactly did I count the Oms if I was breathing in? I should have asked Margaret to intone them, I suppose, but that would have felt too odd, as if we were acting out a parody of a 70s-style play. It might have been attractively simple but it was also deceptively difficult, and it seemed to do no more than empty my lungs of air by the time I got through a few cycles, leaving me gasping. Really, it did nothing for me.

Later I asked Margaret to try the same and she had no

problem with it, although it didn't do anything obvious for her
on inner levels.

However, I wasn't gonna write him off so quickly. After
all, he put out techniques which seemed to work for him, made
no attempt to mystify or suck people into worshipping him, and
was so damned enthusiastic that you had to give him a chance or
two. His second technique involved mentally prostrating myself
at the lotus-feet of the sat-Guru and reciting Sutras in praise of
God and the Guru. Well, I have odd ideas about God(s) and just
didn't want a guru, and I had no sutras (holy verses) to recite,
so I sat in front of my Shakti and tried intoning some half-
remembered poems by Dylan Thomas instead: "As I was young
and easy under the apple boughs ..."

Then, according to the instructions I had to stop and
inhale deeply, without making any sound.

> As you inhale, feel that the Kundalini lying
> dormant in the Muladhara Chakra is
> awakened and is going up from Chakra to
> Chakra. At the conclusion of the Puraka,
> have the Bhavana that the Kundalini has
> reached the Sahasrara. The more vivid the
> visualisation of Chakra after Chakra, the
> more rapid will be your progress in this
> Sachana.
>
> Retain the breath for a short while.
> Repeat the Pranava or your Ishta Mantra.
> Concentrate on the Sahasrara Chakra. Feel
> that by the Grace of Mother Kundalini,
> the darkness of ignorance enveloping your
> soul has been dispelled. Feel that your
> whole being is pervaded by light, power
> and wisdom.
>
> Slowly exhale now. And, as you exhale
> feel that the Kundalini Shakti is gradually
> descending from the Sahasrara, and from
> Chakra to Chakra, to the Muladhara

Chakra.

Now begin the process again.

It is impossible to extol this wonderful Pranayama adequately. It is the magic wand for attaining perfection very quickly. Even a few days practice will convince you of its remarkable glory. Start from today, this very moment.

You can tell from that last paragraph that something deep happened to him, and his excitement is infectious. Only I felt nothing, other than the curious freedom experienced by being able to sit in front of someone I could trust enough to make a tit of myself with, while attempting something bizarre. Also I didn't know the Ishta Mantra, or understood what Puraka, Pranava, Sadhana or Bhavana meant, and didn't really feel the impulse to check them out. So perhaps, in my urge to find a shortcut to enlightenment, I didn't give it the attention it deserved.

On the other hand the next site I visited gave me a series of powerful techniques which did impact. These were written by J. Van. Auken, and I'll give the first of them here, right now, so you too can start today, from this very moment. It is called the 'Strengthening and Opening Breath.'

It begins with a deep inhalation through the right nostril, filling the lungs and feeling strength! Then exhalation through the mouth. This should be felt throughout the torso of the body — STRENGTH! After three of these, shift to inhaling through the left nostril and exhaling through the right (not through the mouth). This time feel the opening of your centers. As you do this left-right nostril breathing, keep your focus on the third eye and crown chakra, letting the other centers open toward these two. This

will not be difficult because the sixth and
seventh centers have a natural magnetism
— just as the snake charmer's music.

*edgarcayce.org/ps2/kundalini_
meditation_J_Van_Auken.html*

I actually tried this sitting in front of the computer screen,
which is not the ideal approach, I'm sure, but, bugger me, I had
that opening-of-the-brow feeling again, a sense of lightness and
not-quite-hereness. Was it merely hyperventilation? Radiations
from the monitor? No, believe me, I'm not so daft that I can't tell
the difference. And by 'lightness' I mean a curious luminescence
as much as lack of weight, as if my true Self was functioning
slightly outside of my body in a brighter world than this.

I didn't actually want to proceed any further just then,
because I wanted to combine it with the Flower Technique, and
try this in tandem with Margaret. But on reading the section
again, I did note the URL, which linked it with the seer of
Virginia Beach, Edgar Cayce, who saw things in the akashic
light in the same way that Blavatsky did.

Which brings me back to the Library or Web Angel
again, the underlying energies of prana and akasha (if there's a
difference) and the curious notion of synchronicity…

Many of us, perhaps most of us, have times in our life
when bizarre sequences of coincidence happen all the time.
In each case, the odds against these coincidences happening
are probably measurable by those mathematics which can
compute in the billions, and they are usually tinged with a
certain 'otherness,' as if unseen powers were at work for reasons
which we can never quite discern. Carl Jung coined the term
'synchronicity,' and we can look at some of the definitions here,
because if you make any attempt to raise your own Kundalini, or
do any sort of work along these lines at all, then the synchronistic
events will flutter into your world like moths to the flame.

Synchronicity is:

- A Jungian term for a meaningful coincidence that has a low probability of being a random or chance event.

  schuelers.com/ChaosPsyche/glossary.htm

- An attempt to explain an apparent relationship between two or more events which have no obvious link. The term was put forward by psychologist Carl Jung (1875-1961) who believed that the positioning of heavenly bodies couldn't have a 'causal' connection with the lives of people on Earth but still felt that the evidence for this astrology was still strong enough for an alternative explanation.

  embassy.org.nz/encycl/s13encyc.htm

- A concept coined by Jung. It denotes a meaningful coincidence or correspondence of two or more outer and inner events. It signifies the meaningful concurrence of a physical and a psychic event which are connected not causally but by meaning.

  bemyastrologer.com/definitionsofjungianterms.html

- Refers to the alignment of forces in the universe to create an event or circumstance.

  indexlistus.de/keyword/List_of_alternative,_speculative_and_ disputed_theories.php

Jung himself gave a perfect example of what this can involve. He wrote about a crisis that occurred during therapy with a woman patient whose highly rational approach to life made any form of treatment extremely difficult. On one occasion, the woman related a dream in which a golden scarab appeared. Jung knew that such a beetle was of great significance to the ancient Egyptians, for it was taken as a symbol of rebirth. As the woman was talking, the psychiatrist in his darkened office heard a tapping at the window behind him. He drew the curtain, opened the window, and in flew a gold-green scarab, called a *rose chafer*, or *Cetonia aureate*. Jung showed the woman 'her' scarab and from that moment the patient's excessive rationality was pierced and their sessions together became more profitable.

This sort of thing will happen to every reader who makes

any attempt to work with the energies of prana and akasha and Kundalini. Trust me, it will. I mean, you won't get scarabs at your window, but you'll certainly stumble into people, books, songs, places and events which will have as much impact, and tantalise you marvelously.

There is even a site devoted to 'meaningful coincidences' which also encourages you to add your own, at *meaningoflife.i12. com/coincidence.htm* Quite apart from the discussion forum it flung up the sort of technique I can never resist, that is not only free but promises the universe. It advises you to read out loud three times the following formula:

> *May the positive forces, whatever be their name, render me worthy of accessing the mysteries of Synchronicity*
> *Here I am; I am ready. Here I am.*
> *I breathe and participate in the wave of the Synchronic moment.*
> *So be it.*

It follows up by advising you in block capitals: BE ALERT, because God (however you think of It) will start to talk to you through symbols, archetypes, weird coincidences, or organized chaos.

Well of course I did it there and then. Three times and one for luck. It seemed to work for me, as I shall soon explain. Go on, try it yourself. Let them know what happens. Drop me a line also, c/o the publishers.

Y'see I just had the idea that prana, the Shakti, the Kundalini, and the energies involved in synchronicity were all one and the same. Had I actually reached this viewpoint through intuition, brought on by the few exercises I had tried so far? Was it something remembered from my vast reading in bygone years? Was it merely something I had glimpsed in the endless pages I had downloaded or studied on-line? Probably the latter, to be honest. Well, does it matter where the perception comes from as long as it has some truth?

As to prana, the sages at *upnaway.com/~bindu/windsong/ terms.htm* commented: "Striking a relationship with prana itself is difficult but is often established when prana introduces itself prior to, during, or after (even days or weeks after) a classical Kundalini awakening." I had no problem with the notion or visualisation of the stuff: was I on track for rattling good arousal? Would any of this affect Margaret too?

From what I had learned so far, and started to experience, it appears that when you begin to swirl the pranic energies in your body and soul, you are swirling the energies of the universe. Things — synchronistic events — will naturally be drawn toward your life, like flotsam in a vortex. Perhaps it was the effect of all the breathing exercises, the linking with the concept and actuality of prana, the tickling of the Kundalini consciousness; or perhaps it was simply the formulaic prayer mentioned above which did the trick, but odd things started to happen in Margaret's life in ways that I cannot really explain. Not because they are beyond my powers of description, but because she'd have my balls off if I blabbed. Suffice to say that synchronistic events involving Christine Hartley impacted in her life in a completely unexpected way.

Remember, I said in the preface that Christine had been Shakti to a man named Charles 'Kim' Seymour in the late 1930s, and that in many ways she inspired this whole Google Tantra project. But Christine (who died in 1985) was *my* teacher! Margaret had never even heard of her before. Why didn't Christine, who was a truly great soul, come through to me in the bizarre and must-be-kept-secret way that she did to Margaret? Hey, I'll admit it, I was a teensy bit jealous. As for the way the synchronistic events touched my life at this time, who or what did I get, eh?

I got Aunty Winny, sans the carrot-sized wodges of cotton wool. And no, I'm not labouring a joke here. It happened like this ...

We went to a spiritualist church one Saturday evening. Although I'm not a spiritualist, or a Christian, I've got a lot of time for these excellent folk who, week in and week out, put their unusual talents on the line by standing up before complete strangers and attempting to demonstrate that there is no death. They put themselves in the firing line of serious, potentially devastating fusillades of hope, fear, disappointment, sheer scornful disbelief and often pitiable despair. That must take some nerve. They are easy targets, mediums. To outsiders and sceptics, the messages they offer can seem banal, derisory, but the effect upon the recipient is so often profound. When I am dead, if I've got a few minutes to come back through a medium and try to pass on a message to my children, it won't be deeply philosophical: First, I'll prove who I am by giving them some memory of something we shared that no-one else will know about; and then I'll tell them that I still love them, and always will.

So although I've seen a few mediums that I can best describe as 'weak,' I've never met a phoney. By and large the visiting mediums leave audiences moved and consoled - and all for the price of a cup of tea. That takes some commitment.

The church itself, near the centre of the small and rather battered looking town of Melksham, was built by Quakers, but has existed as a centre of Spiritualist excellence for many decades now. It's a strong sort of place with the air of an old and trusted overcoat: it fits nicely around as you enter; it's heavy and will keep you from storms. I was reminded of the brief poem called A Coat by W.B. Yeats (1865–1939) which goes:

> I made my song a coat
> Covered with embroideries
> Out of old mythologies
> From heel to throat;
> But the fools caught it,
> Wore it in the world's eyes
> As though they'd wrought it.
> Song, let them take it
> For there's more enterprise
> In walking naked.
> *bartleby.com/147/31.html*

And I was further reminded that Yeats, no mean psychic

himself, once wrote about the spirits which came to him saying: *We have come to bring you new metaphors for poetry.* And they did, and he used them, and he got the Nobel Prize for it all. Though I doubt if he'd ever been to Melksham Spiritualist Church, except inside a poem that rattled briefly inside my head.

Margaret had only been to such a place once before, and that too had been at my urging. On that visit she had been nervous, not sure what to expect, half-imagining that the medium would go into the sort of trance you would get on the old Hammer Horror Films, which involved lolling tongues, rolling eyes, glimpses of nipples, and was clearly one spasm removed from demonic possession. In the event she had been both surprised and charmed by the suited young man from Swindon who gave her some meaningful advice from a spirit whom she felt was her mum. This time, she was positively blasé.

As for me, well I sometimes go to these churches, using them as a kind of *poste restante*, hoping for some tangible guidance from the Otherworld. Once I'd raised my Kundalini I wouldn't need to do this, but for the time being I felt that I still needed a middle-man ... or a medium.

I suppose if you had clairvoyant sight that night, I would have looked like a firework party. This was because I tried to do all sorts of mental games with the visiting medium to get a message for myself or Margaret. I actually think that the man who sat on the platform behind the lady medium could see what I was trying to do because he kept giving me odd and uncomfortable looks as I ...

- Did the Flower technique, opening the chakras
- Circulated force through my aura
- Visualised a gaudy neon star above my head to get the medium's attention
- Visualised myself as being gigantic
- Visualised gigantic me grabbing her head and slapping it about a bit, turning it to look in my direction
- Reversed all of these, visualised myself standing small

and humbly before her, saying *Please* …

God. I was inwardly exhausted when the woman (one half of a husband and wife team from Portsmouth) turned to me and said: I've got someone here called Winny … before going on to describe her with reasonable accuracy of form and farming background, but no substance in terms of message. Well I had to laugh, inwardly. To tell you the truth Aunty Winny has never figured large in my life at all. I've used her in a cowardly sort of way to avoid targeting my Mam, *The Mam*, who was Ashington's answer to Kali, the Dark and Destroying Goddess. Aunty Winny was just an empty shell in my memories, without impact or substance, and that's the way she came across just then, just picked off the surface of my aura as a kind of in-joke offered by the spirits.

But then the medium turned her vision on Margaret and she was spot-on, in depth, evidential. I won't give details because they would seem trivial to an outsider, in the ways described above. Suffice to say that in that large hall in a small town in the heart of rural Wiltshire, Margaret from Brussels felt herself surrounded by family and concerned spirits, and truly loved. And when the medium told us that we seemed to be two halves of one soul then we both felt really pleased. Shiva and Shakti. Yang and Yin. Tantrickas?

Well, perhaps not yet.

84

Chapter 5

There is one energy (Shakti) that keeps taking on new shapes and forms. Each time the energy takes on a new form, we give it a new name. Shakti becomes Kundalini Shakti, or simply Kundalini. Kundalini becomes Prana, which flows in Nadis, and concentrates itself in Chakras. The subtle energies condense and become known as earth, water, fire, air, and space in the gross world. With Kundalini awakening, the primal energy of Shakti awakens in its true form.

Swami Jnaneshvara Bharati
swamij.com/ shakti.htm

Not long ago I could have read the above

and – echoing my old hard-of-hearing Dad – would have said a loud EH?! But it made sense now by breaking it down into simple English: there is a universal energy which flows through everything. It is accessible in some places more than others. This energy which flows through us as human beings is the same as the energy which flows through the material world around and the spiritual equivalent within. At least I think that's what the

Swami was saying. I felt that my own quest to find and raise the Kundalini might be more effective if I got out a bit more, and gave the pixels a rest.

One of the earlier sites I visited in Chapter 2, and I mean Internet here, not geographical, said that in certain places the solar prana, air prana and ground prana, are more prevalent than in others. Some of these highly energized areas tend to become healing centres. I wanted to see if practicising some of the techniques in a recognised holy place and healing centre would give them an extra clout. So I did what any sane Englishman always does when the sun shines: I lured Margaret out into the glorious countryside to try and show her delights she could never find in the Opus Dei-ridden lairs of Brussels, hoping at some point she might have sex with me out of doors.

It was a gorgeous day, May 1st, the ancient Celtic feast day of Beltaine. Before I made the sandwiches, I tapped the word Beltaine into Google to see what I could glean about it. According to Sig Lonegren at *geomancy.org/quarter&cross/beltane. html* this is the day when "The seed, which was planted last November at Samhain (Sow-an), and moved all by itself for the first time in February at Imbolc, is now up and growing. For the Celts, this was a time of fertility. The May Pole's phallic shape is but a mild hint at the kind of spring revels that went on during this day and night sacred to the Sun God Bel. ..."

Beltaine, then, is a time of fertility, as expressed by the phallus. Lonegren asks: "What part of your life is particularly fertile, particularly ready to grow? Is there a place inside you that's saying, 'Hey, I really want to spend more time doing _____.'? Take advantage of the energy of this time. Use Fire to energize you for the growth ahead." Well, I knew what I wanted in that respect: the Serpent Fire. Maybe it would ignite on Beltaine? Would it matter that I had had a vasectomy? Can changes in the body affect the spirit in the same way that changes in spirit are said to affect the body?

"Where did you hear that?" asked Margaret, referring to that last bit.

I Googled my own memory banks. I got no hits. And it took so long that Margaret smelled a decomposing rat: "You just made that up didn't you?"

I suppose I did.

So we went to Chalice Orchard at the foot of Glastonbury Tor. I'm never quite sure if it's a deeply holy place with some modern, mawkish additions, or something of a New Age miniature theme park which has been built upon a deep and underlying sanctity. It has a virtual tour on its web site at: *chalicewell.org.uk* so if you want to go there now and see what I'm trying to describe, you might appreciate it better.

There is: a modern pool shaped in the form of a *vesica piscis* on the open lawn to which the waters descend through flow forms; an old oblong pool in what they call King Arthur's Courtyard, through which major ley lines apparently course, which is approached by a door above which Excalibur is seen. Both of these are fed by the spring water pouring out of the spout known as the Lion's Head from which the daily flow of spring water is about 25,000 gallons, and beyond which are the holy thorns said to originate from the staff of Joseph of Arimithea when he visited England with his nephew; plus various peaceful nooks and crannies which sort of radiate out from the undoubtedly numinous Chalice Well.

"These waters are tinged red by chalybeate," I told Margaret knowingly, as we bent over the Lion's Head and filled one of the glasses that they leave out for pilgrims.

"What's chalybeate?" she asked, sipping and pulling a face, then sipping some more on the principle that anything so foul must be good. Well I was ready for her cunning mind games, having already looked up everything possible before we left, at *en.wikipedia.org/wiki/Chalybeate*

"Chalybeate, my precious, means simply 'containing or impregnated with or tasting of iron.' Do you know that from early in the 17th century, chalybeate water was said to have health-giving properties and many people promoted their qualities? Why, old Lord North's physician, for example, claimed that it contained vitriol and, according to opinion of the day, could cure the colic, the melancholy, and the vapours; it made the lean fat, the fat lean; it killed flat worms in the belly, loosened the clammy humours of the body, and dried the over-moist brain."

"Hmmm …" she answered, giving me a look. "What's all this got to do with Serpent Powers?"

Well forgive me if I snort here. Y'see to be honest, there weren't really any cosmic impulses behind our visit, and believe me Serpent Powers were the last thing on her mind when we set out. As for me, I'm not one of those who regard Glastonbury as the Heart Chakra of the universe, and if I never see another shop selling crystals and plastic angels, or High Priestesses offering Goddess workshops again I'll be well pleased. In fact my well-worn battle-cry 'Glastonbury is for sissies' just about sums up my attitude toward the town. No, we went simply because I like picnics, and Margaret likes gardens, and it's a sheltered place on the way to the small town of Street, which is to shoes what Brussels is to chocolate. And Margaret likes shoes possibly even more than she likes gardens and chocolate. And if I could combine it all, then …

"Look at that tree!" she said, interrupting my spleen before I dared to try and show it. She has a strange affinity with trees, and has hugged more than a few in that coy, left-of-centre, mittel-European way of hers. I knew exactly which one she meant and inwardly glowed. This was an heroic English yew, the sort from which the mighty Robin Hood would have made his mighty bow in those mighty forests of Sherwood which surround boyhoods everywhere, and greater (I was sure) than any of the mythologically unformed growths she might find in the Jean-Claude van Dammed wastelands around Brussels. The yew is one of the oldest living things on the planet, and was a sacred tree to just about everyone from the time of the Big Bang onwards – or, in Egyptian terms, from the moment when the creator-god Atum masturbated the universe into existence. This one, just up the hill from the Vesica Pool is an old yew tree that has grown apart at the base and then grown together again higher up, creating a vulvic shape that everyone, just everyone, knows is sacred to the Goddess, and which has the tinged waters as her blood spring. Archaeologists found the remains of a 2000 year old yew stump near the Chalice Well itself, and it is likely that there was a processional pathway of yews in ancient times. Try to visualise this, and the image springs up very easily.

I took her hand, using my Grip of Power to drag her past the living yoni before she tried to do embarrassing things, and we found the circular area around the well deserted, almost humming with the sort of energised calm that I associate with great cathedrals, and which this small space probably is, on inner levels.

The keepers themselves write:

> Since ancient times, the waters that flow from deep below our planet have been revered as the essence of life, the gift of mother earth to sustain all her living forms. A spring such as the Chalice Well which has never been known to fail is especially revered as a symbol of the continuous and unbounded nature of the life force. The people of old saw the wells as gateways to the spirit world where the veils between human existence and the greater spirit became thinner, and communications could take place with the gods and goddesses of the nature religions.

"The cover of the well," I told her, quoting verbatim, "is English Oak, surmounted by a wrought iron vesica piscis, with the 'bleeding lance,' passing through it. This was donated by the archaeologist, Frederick Bligh Bond in 1919. He had a great interest in sacred geometry, and was the resident archeologist at the abbey for several years." I pointed out also the phallic and yonic symbolism inherent in both the patterned cover and the well itself.

She didn't answer. She was staring into the depths of the well as so many have done over so many centuries. I had one of my 'feeling like a twat' moments and shut up, sitting next to her on the inlaid stone bench. I was struck once again by how lovely she was – is! – and how much fun, and how lucky I was – am! Ashington and my Nobby No-Friends days seemed a very long way away, in another dimension beyond time, space and brown ale.

On an impulse I left her side and knelt over the well, looking inside for the chamber of 'Egyptian proportions' mentioned on the web-site, but I couldn't make it out. Yet I had the sense that I had to reach through the mesh and touch the waters. For a brief second the title and image of Dali's painting Adoration of Narcissus came to mind, and then that was replaced with an image of myself, touching the waters, as if I were my own reflection (which I probably am, in Buddhist terms), and then I had another very fleeting sense of entities within the well, within the waters, looking out at me.

I sat back with Margaret and ate the silence. She held my hand. When I asked her later what she had felt at that moment, in that place, she confessed:

"I felt that I should be pure and holy, and not think pervy thoughts. What was in your mind?"

"I was hoping you'd get my dick out," I said.

That was not as absurd, rude or as scatological as it may sound: I have heard a number of people confess that ancient sites can invoke in them what might be termed a 'horny as hell' feeling. In fact that term itself is almost exquisitely apt, considering the influence of the ancient Horned God and Goddess at the pre-Christian (pre-everything) holy places. It may be something to do with picking up inner echoes of the fertility rites. It may be more to do with falling in tune with the 'cosmic fuck' energies mentioned earlier, and which D. H. Lawrence captured so beautifully in that section from The Rainbow, in which people who worked the land felt: "… the pulse and body of the soil, that opened to their furrow for the grain, and became smooth and supple after their ploughing, and clung to their feet with a weight that pulled like desire, lying hard and unresponsive when the crops were to be shorn away."

I don't know too many who have confessed to the same in churches or the great cathedrals, but maybe stone does something else to the energies which some of them undoubtedly channel. So if the whole universe really is just one un-ending fuck, then at places where the veil between the worlds is thin it is natural that we resonate to such impulses. And what better time to feel this than Beltaine?

I had to calm those feelings and their uncomfortable and often embarrassing physical responses *asap* if we wanted to press on, so I did what every man should do in such a situation: I spent some time thinking about the insanity of Shola Ameobi playing on the left wing for Newcastle United.

Well that worked in seconds, and we moved to a different part of the orchard and sat on a bench next to a large wicker figure, with the overshadowing Tor to one side, and looking across to the house where Serpent Fires were once raised by the late great Dion Fortune, who did some of her best magick there, and changed the world in doing so.

"That's where Serpent Fires were once raised by the late great Dion Fortune, who did some of her best magick there, and changed the world in doing so," I proffered.

" I wish you'd stop keep reading from your notes. And you're not going to lecture me again about her being the Shakti of the Age are you?" Margaret asked, seeing my eyes go a bit misty and my body language alter quite drastically as it always does when DF is mentioned – always by me.

"Hey listen, *ecoutez*, type 'Dion Fortune' into Google and you'll get 180,000 hits in 0.20 seconds. I think that deserves a little respect, *hein*?"

She nodded. She knew better than to stop a runaway train. She also knew that it's best to humour lunatics. Honestly, she's dead smart is my Shakti.

But while we're at this place and on this topic, did the blessed Dion Fortune really have any direct experience of the traditional Tantra? To my astonishment Google had found me the following, by Shahindran Moonieya, in an article entitled

'Tantra: A Way of Life and a System of Magick.'

> A pertinent fact that many of us are not aware of, is that the great founders of contemporary witchcraft and the thinkers of the contemporary pagan world viz; Dionne Fortune [sic], Blavatsky, Gardiner [sic] and many others all studied the Tantric texts. Very few people know or acknowledge the fact that Dionne Fortune and others all corresponded with and were intimately acquainted with Swami Lakshmanjoo, who lived from 1907 to 1994. The Swami was a master of both the practical and theoretical dimensions of the Hindu Tantra.
>
> *cam.za.net/about/paths/tantra.html*

Well I thought I knew some stuff about Our Vi, as I call her, but I didn't know that! Nor was the writer able to go into more detail when I sent a rapid email. But Shahindran (to my slight embarrassment I don't know if it's a he or she) was certainly correct in the later paragraph with the comment that much of the current transliteration and interpretation in Western Paganism is down to Dion Fortune, Blavatsky, Gerald Gardner, the Theosophical Society, "… and other such early western explorers into the maze of the Eastern Occultism and Esoteric." The writer goes on to note that "… the late Swami Lakshmanjoo [1907 – 1994] who was the great Tantric master of the Kaula tradition of the Hindu Tantric tradition of Kashmir … was one of a few Hindu masters who agreed to work with Western Scholars. A little known fact is that he was well acquainted with Dion Fortune. The dynamics of that relationship would have been a marvel to behold."

Listen … if anyone out there can add anything pertinent, then they should write to me via the publishers at any hour of the day or night. I Googled Swami Lakshmanjoo and I think I fell in love with his picture. When I grow up I want to look as benign as him.

But I avoided getting too drawn into the Swami and the associated links because I knew that Chalice Well was coming up, and I wanted something practical and healthy and not radiating from the monitor of a PC.

"Alan ..." she whispered, and I could tell from the pregnant nature of those three dots that I'd better get on with the next technique there and then.

In this crowded world, not many people make the effort or even have the opportunity to be able to sit in a beautiful and holy place without having to worry about being mugged or having your handbag stolen just as the prana rises in your left nostril. Even so I made sure where my wallet was then sort of glanced around with my left eye and right brain, trying to suss out any dodgy characters before I closed both and got down to it.

"Close your eyes," I said as we sat side by side on the small bench. "Now relax, breathe in a steady rhythm and visualise your body filling with light at each inbreath."

The technique I found, by Googling the words 'inner fire' is given by the magician and musician R.J. Stewart *atdreampower. com/rising_light.html.* It involves visualising a source of energy just below the ground, like a flowing and glowing ball of light. The upper surface of this energy sphere touches the soles of your feet, and from its lower surface a thin cord of light, like an umbilical, descends toward the core of the planet, where it links with a hitherto unknown energy source.

"Be aware of this energy sphere, and feel it touching you. Move your imagination into it. You may feel your own energies descending into it. Now try and draw the energy source up and into yourself ..."

Read the technique for yourself. Browse his site and buy some CDs, and study his take on the four zones of the body/energy field which does away with chakras entirely and substitutes: Feet (Earth), Genitals (Water), Heart (Fire), and Throat/Head (Air). Muse on his descriptions of the feelings that you might experience as you bring the energies up through these zones, and realise that you don't have to do the chakra thing. You don't have to do anything blindly.

Sometimes I think that it doesn't matter what you do, or what system you believe in, as long you try something, and as long as it's original to you. Certainly when it comes to doing these exercises you don't need to feel an immediate response … it's more a matter of telling the unconscious that you're doing something different, unusual, and the unconscious takes it from there, often using synchronicity in the outer world as the first response, plus vivid and intense, and usually totally meaningless dreams.

So we sat there in the Chalice Orchard and tried to work with our inner fires, and I can only say that 'things fell away' as we sat there. Whether it was the cares of the world or my bodily stresses relaxing under the warmth, the company and the bird song, wasn't important.

"Where were you?" asked Margaret when we both stopped the exercise and brought ourselves back into the orchard.

As if arousing from deep sleep it took me a while to answer. I had felt as if I were on a height. On top of a steep cliff. It was a sense of actual location with a vivid rolling green landscape stretching away before me. But it was certainly not anywhere in Somerset. Even though a large part of my consciousness never lost track of the fact that I was sitting on a bench in Chalice Orchard, somehow I was also perched atop this cliff with a feeling that I could project myself astrally any time I had the nerve to jump. I didn't have the nerve.

"Or something like that," I finished lamely.

The experience of the day led on to an unusually intense dream in the night. I dream a lot and remember much, but I've never believed that they are necessarily significant. According to Marc Ian Barasch:

> Many cultures have had a terminology
> for such dreams of surpassing power.

The Greek New Testament seems to contain more words for inner experience than Eskimos have for snow: onar (a vision seen in sleep as opposed to waking); enypnion (a vision seen in sleep that comes by surprise); horama (which could refer to visions of the night, sleeping visions, or waking visions); horasis (a supernatural vision); optasia (a supernatural vision that implies the Deity revealing Himself); and so on. By and large the English language has been impoverished of a working vocabulary; we have little at hand beyond dream and nightmare. Given our cultural paucity, it can be a struggle to define these signal occurrences.

gracecathedral.org/enrichment/excerpts/exc_20010718.shtml

Taking the simple approach of the Ashington Lad, I class my dreams as pure bollocks caused by a sort of jiggling together and then emptying of the recycle bin at the end of the day, or as Big Ones, which seem to be marked by a certain intensity and clarity. I think this might have been a Big One ...

I dreamt I was on a car journey with Margaret, somewhere in western Europe. It was pitch black, sometime before dawn, and while she stayed in the car and slept I felt compelled to get out and look around. Suddenly it became as bright as day, two stunningly bright pulses of illumination, and I wondered if this was caused by nuclear explosions, even though I had heard no sound. Then, as if realising what was happening, Margaret started the car and came across to get me ahead of some rapidly rising water. She drove up and up until we came to a small village perched on the edge of a hill where the roads were all blocked by other cars, and we had to abandon ours. An old lady came out of her house and invited us in. To Margaret's delight and astonishment the woman was a Flemish speaker.

and as the sun rose I left them alone while I went to the edge of the hill and looked out over the land. Instead of green fields it was all now sea, and the other villagers were coming to terms with what was obviously a global catastrophe or at very least a local one on an immense scale, with bridges down, whole cities flooded, countless lives lost, and with no communications via phone, television or any other medium. It was a clear End of the World dream.

I don't know where this was. It could have been on the edges of Somerset, looking westward toward the Bristol Channel, because after all those lands had been reclaimed from the sea over the millennia and it wouldn't take much to overwhelm the various natural and artificial sea-gates. Or it could have been somewhere on the edges of the Low Countries – hence the unexpected Flemish-speaking woman as a clue.

Now water is a classic and universal symbol for the unconscious mind so, was all this just a surge from my own depths, stimulated as they must have been by the various exercises? Or was it genuinely prophetic insight, as you are supposed to get when the Kundalini starts to awaken? How much of this had to do with the sacred centre of Chalice Orchard? If you look at the traditions, this was certainly a place that resonated to the notion of the Shakti – all those priestesses who served here when the lands surrounding it were as underwater as my dream.

In my notes I had jotted down: "Relevance: some places have more prana, the akasha as feminine, the earth as source of energy, water as life, prana as life ..." Would it be easier to raise the Serpent Power when visiting a site like this? Or would the beast raise its head just as willingly in my little flat in the middle of the concrete wastes of a small Wiltshire town? The only way to test this would be to visit some other site which might be expected to 'have more prana,' and decided upon Stoney Littleton long barrow.

Google found more than enough entries for this place, although the most direct is probably *stonepages.com/england/ stoneylittleton.htm* where it describes the barrow as follows:

Probably the most interesting chambered long barrow in south-western England, Stoney Littleton is about 30m (98ft) long, 15m (49ft) broad and 2.7m (9ft) high ...

The stone chambers lie at the south-eastern end of the long grassy mound, the horns of which create a fore court in front of the entrance. It is thought that corpses lay first in the entrance passage, only being moved into the chambers when decay had completed. The entrance leads to a 16m (52ft) gallery with three pairs of side chambers and an end chamber. The passage is very narrow, and only 1.2m (4ft) high in places...

A fine fossil ammonite decorates the left-hand door jamb with a spiral; the spiral is a symbol used by various cultures to represent the passage through life and death.

Plus there is a whole collection of rave reviews and neat little pictures at *megalithic.co.uk/article.php?sid=421* where you can see that this little hollow bump in the ground has touched an awful lot of people, most of whom are rather troubled by the fact that the place has finally been discovered by the New Age tossers with their crystals and their smudge sticks, chanting and drumming their way toward a new dispensation of all-embracing niceness. A kind of *Nicianity*, if you can imagine such a hell.

And to my astonishment I also found a QTVR tour of the site created by Pete Glastonbury. Now I have no idea what that stands for and have even less interest in anyone writing to tell me. My astonishment sprang from the fact that if you 'gripped' the picture by holding down the left button of the mouse you could look 360° around the inside and the outside of the long barrow. Not as good as being there, of course, as it doesn't capture the atmosphere, but better than a jab on your ajna with a cold pendulum. So if you can't get there in person and want the next best thing, get your mouse-finger warmed up and go to: *stonehenge-avebury.net/Photos/gtour/QtvrtourAve10.html*

When we visited Stoney Littleton it was as much to do with having our own 'rebirth' ceremony as me trying to raise the serpent power. Not that the latter was inconsistent with the long barrow, because Google had also found me many associations between barrows and dragons. In Germanic epic poetry such as Beowulf, for example, barrows were widely perceived as the houses of these primeval winged serpents which fly through the dreams and nightmares of our oldest time.

David Yarrow in his excellent and healthy essay 'Power of the Earth Spirit' writes about the esoteric aspect of dragons and comments:

> Modern geophysical science tells us the planet is enfolded in a magnetic field within which flow vast electromagnetic currents arising from entrapped solar radiation and impulses surging deep in the Earth. Dragon is a concept to define how impulses of the planetary energy field are stored up here and flow out there as channels and pools of terrestrial electromagnetism. To see a dragon is to perceive the channels of subtle natural energy at the planet's surface. The dragon's body is defined by the physical features of the land where these invisible telluric currents circulate and collect.

> *championtrees.org/yarrow/dragons.htm*

Reading this and comparing it with all that had gone before, it seemed that the diversities of the Kundalini/serpent/chakra/energy/prana/shakti/earth-consciousness was nothing more than different coloured aspects of the same thing. I wanted to find and awaken the serpent within me. But maybe this was intimately connected with finding and awakening the dragon energies within the land.

To Gloria Joy Greco at *kundalini-gateway.org* the "Kundalini is the sleeping dragon within the body that is to be brought into action when all soul preparation is accomplished. There is a time and place for its awakening, it is not meant to be manipulated or forced in anyway."

Others have equated the Western caduceus with its entwined serpents, and also the Eastern columns of the ida and the pingala spiralling around the central sushumna, to the double helix of DNA, which they feel the ancients had intuitively discerned. There are the intriguing comments from the wonderfully named 'Mystress Angelique Serpent' who notes on her website that these fire serpents are your own DNA strands. She writes with confidence and aplomb:

> Kundalini is the Fire Serpent, you can think of the Fire Serpent as the spirit of DNA. DNA emits light like a telsa coil emits electricity. Your DNA is a very complex mechanism. If you took all of your DNA from out of your cells, and unfolded it, unpacked it from its tightly coiled state as a double helix, it would stretch all the way to the sun and back again. Now, if you could think of something like that, a magnetic tape that stretches all the way to the sun and back again, and how much information you could put on that tape, then you're getting some limited idea of exactly how much information is available through your own DNA.
>
> Some of that information is gonna unfold as the serpents unfold. You're

going to start getting information from
your body that may not necessarily be
in words, but it will be information.
Some people who go through Kundalini
actually experience memories of their
grandparents, particularly on the female
side. Women may get memories of being
their great great-grandmother. I've had
memories of being my grandfather, when
he was an officer.

domin8rex.com/serpent/spirit/serpent.htm

I realise now that this was perhaps crucial to my present
quest, and understanding of certain things have happened
to myself, and I think we'll come back to Mystress Angelique
later.

Yet in truth, it wasn't so much dragons we wanted at
this moment but the rebirthing aspect: the coming-forth-from-
darkness, because this was the month in both of our lives when,
in the past before we met, everything had turned into shite. So I
suppose, in a sense, taking away the crystals, smudge sticks, and
drums, we weren't much different to the New Agers that the
bloggers moaned about.

The barrow is approached down a long road just wide
enough for my car, followed by a short steep walk across a
faery bridge and then up over the fields to the hill crest where
it stands. Or lurks rather. Not that it is in any way sinister, but
more like a person lying down in the grass of a hilltop, watching
out over the world below. I had a huge urge to hurry there,
and impressed Margaret with my *lung-gom-pa* stride, explaining
to her all about the running lamas of Tibet that my dear old
chum Lobsang used to write about. She was panting too much
to riposte.

It was a different sort of atmosphere to the orchard:
that was enclosed, this was opened out. If it affected the prana,
then it might show in the techniques I planned to practice. As
we approached the barrow – like a prominent clit, as Margaret

described it – we saw a hawk upon a gate post.

"That's a symbol of Horus, Merlin and Herne the Hunter" I told her, deeply pleased with this omen. There was a huge three-quarter moon low in the sky and lots of horned slugs around and we both spent some time honouring the people who had built this, for reasons no-one could really say. We sat on the top feeling a deep stillness that was broken only briefly when a scruffy black dog appeared, followed by its green-wellied owner.

"That's also a symbol of Horus, Merlin and Herne the Hunter," I said. "The dog, I mean, not the prat in the hat." I gave the latter a Look of Power and he went.

Margaret lay on her stomach and wept for no reason but the peace of it all. I lay next to her on my back and watched the sky, and almost felt myself falling into it. This was not a place for psycho-spiritual techniques, and we didn't even feel horny. Then we sat within the darkness of the barrow and watched the moon framed by the entrance, and the hawk flew back and forth across that sacred space and made us feel a little blessed. I'm not sure any Master of Serpent Fires would have gone into alternate-nostril breathing mode and spoiled what that barrow was giving us then. If this is what R.J. Stewart meant by 'earth-peace' then we were blessed indeed.

As we left, my watch just fell off my wrist where the spindle had come away. It hadn't caught on anything, and I was lucky to have noticed. I think it was the faeries trying to exact a gift, even though we had brought them some Guiness. Stupidly, I fixed it and put it back on.

When we came back home that night Margaret cooked me some toast, scraped off the burnt bits (all of it) and showed me a letter I had written to her 20 years before, after our own young and brief two-ships-passing-in-the-night (or more accurately crashing-in-the-linen-cupboard) fling had come to an affectionate end and we had gone our very separate ways. I was quite moved to read it. I think I was teetering on the edge of love with her even then – more than I was able to admit or even allow.

"This is more important than Serpent Fires," she said, snuggling into me under the covers while the rain came down outside, and I loved her so much I didn't even want to have sex. I had to agree.

I mentioned the incident with the watch because synchronicity kicked in again. As I went to the local library the next day, I saw the splendidly lurid cover of a book called *Sex and Rockets* by John Carter almost leering at me from New Books shelf. It's an excellent biography of Jack Parsons, one-time friend and room-mate of L.Ron Hubbard, follower of Aleister Crowley and an influential figure in the early history of American rocketry. Opening it at random, the following leapt out at me:

> "'I [Aleister Crowley] have noticed that every time I receive an important initiation, some cherished article mysteriously disappears. It may be a pipe, a pen or what not: but it is always an object which is impregnated with my personality by constant use or special veneration. I cannot remember a single occasion when this has not happened. The theory is that the elementals or familiar spirits in attendance on the Magician exact, so to speak, a tip on all important occasions of rejoicing." In such magical workings, evidently, if you don't offer something to the spirits, they will take it anyway ...'

They didn't get the watch at Stoney Littleton but it seems they tried. Exactly a week later when I was in Brussels, deliberately invoking the faeries in Margaret's large garden, it disappeared in bewildering circumstances that are too tedious to relate in detail, but hugely surprising (and exciting) in reality. We both thought of that moment only a few days before when the long barrow had almost claimed the same object. Clearly the unelected bureaucrats of Brussels who rob us blind in fiscal and political areas, have taught their spiritual counterparts lessons which their English faery cousins have yet to master.

Now the point of all this is simple. Working in the realms of the Serpent Fire, at places that are likely to be more numinous than others, seemed to have triggered intense dreams, synchronistic experiences, and moments of quiet bliss. Whether this is to do with making proper use of prana, akasha, shakti energies and the Kundalini, or more a matter of having some nice days out in beautiful places with a beautiful woman and getting some fresh air along the way is not really important. In my slow and gentle efforts toward raising the Kundalini, things were happening that − by every account − were supposed to happen.

I looked back at the many 'Kundalini dangers' described earlier, such as: muscle twitches, cramps or spasms, energy rushes or immense electricity circulating the body, itching, vibrating, prickling, tingling, stinging or crawling sensations, involuntary bodily movements, alterations in eating and sleeping patterns, intensified sexual desires, digestive system problems, numbness or pain in the limbs, pains and blockages anywhere, not to mention emotional outbursts, rapid mood shifts, seemingly unprovoked or excessive episodes of grief, fear, rage, and deep depression ...

Well, I wasn't getting more than a couple dozen of these symptoms on any given day. Leastways nothing that couldn't be controlled by: sitting on my hands, spraying my bits with Daktarin, taking my vitamins after slapping my legs to get the blood flowing, making mad passionate love to Margaret in a gentle sort of way, eating lots of roughage and taking my slow-release Vitamin C, or else biting on my kaftan whenever I felt the slightest tendency toward grief, fear, rage, depression.[6]

As I wrote this I heard a soft wind in my ear, like the breath of a goddess. It was warm, it was lovely. Which of my

6. He doesn't have a kaftan - *Margaret*

favourite goddesses was trying to communicate… Hathor?
Nepthys? Arianrhod? Bride? Nah, even better it was Margaret
leaning over my shoulder to read this, shoving her firm left
breast into my right ear and giving a Euro-sigh at what she felt
was my crassness.

"Do you have to do that?" she asked.

I took my hand from out of her jumper and said nothing.
I was sad. She had to go back to Brussels and it would be some
weeks before she could return. I was getting used to my shakti
being around. Who was I gonna stimulate chakras and circulate
prana with now, or accompany to the Halls of Akasha during
sleep, or have shared magickal and synchronistic experiences in
the tawdry streets of my unexceptional town? The Kundalini
exercises were all very well and effective – so far – but she was
making the mundane magickal, the ordinary into something
exceptional.

"I don't want you to go," I said, looking at the screen of
the computer, not wanting to put pressure on her to stay.

"I have to go," she answered, with the gentlest of
touches.

And so she went. And I felt lonely again. But at least
had my serpent to play with until she returned.

Chapter 6

Waking the Kundalini is simple. Just move the prana down and the apana up until they meet and combine.

realization.org/page/doc0/doc0000.htm

In my daily job in the outer world, to which I apply myself with reasonable conscience but no passion, I tend to live by two maxims: Saki's, which says that "A little inaccuracy sometimes saves tons of explanation," and Bertrand Russell's which insists that "One of the symptoms of an approaching nervous breakdown is the belief that one's work is terribly important." Opinions seem to be divided as to whether I'm cynical about things or just a realist, laid back or simply a bit of a tosser.

Like questors for the Holy Grail I've always needed things to aspire toward, whether it's gurus, heroes (real or in fillums), or spiritual concepts. Sometimes I can get some direction from snappy little wisdoms, cracker-barrel philosophies that can keep others amused or – more often than not – irritated. There's a whole web site of such wisdom alphabetically arranged at *wiseoldsayings.com/wosdirectorya1.htm* and if you're in the mood for amusement you might also like to tap into Google "Facts Of Life — Or Things I've Learned From The Movies" and see if you can find what I did.

In my curious 'otherlife' outside of work and within myself, I long ago realised that high spiritual attainment, such as raising the Kundalini, didn't necessarily mean that the mystic or magus in question was also a highly developed, greater-than-ordinary human being. (And honestly, when it comes to advanced spiritual teachers I've met some real shits in my time. They speak very highly of me too. Plus, genuinely advanced spiritual beings don't have to know a damned thing about Kundalinis or chakras or auras, or even have the slightest interest in them. In fact, taking away the rose-coloured aura goggles, the filters of hero-worship, wish-fulfillment, transference and projection, some of the wisest, kindest, most balanced and effective human beings I've ever known have been ex-miners from Ashington.)

I think that I first read about someone raising the Kundalini in one of Paul Brunton's books which I stumbled upon in Ashington library, and he was my hero for many years until I began to suspect that he was making much of it up. By that time, thanks to being innoculated at any early age by Lobsang Hoskins/Cyril Rampa, I didn't succumb to paralysis, self-doubt and the Dark Night of the Soul. Anyone who still reveres Brunton should Google themselves a copy of 'My Father's Guru: a journey through spirituality and disillusion' by Jeffrey Moussaieff Masson, who more or less grew up with the rascal. According to Brunton, inheriting the attitudes that were common at the time, sexuality and spirituality were mutually opposed. You could not have both.

What a prig. What a phoney. When he wasn't meditating he must have been chewing that carpet mentioned earlier, which we all have known.

So I wanted now to find some account of someone who unquestionably had raised the elusive inner reptile, and it didn't take me long to find Gopi Krishna. Type that name into the search-box and you'll get around 51,800 hits in 0.25 seconds. If anyone has set the benchmark for Kundalini-raising then it is he.

There is a neat biography of him at *om-guru.com/html/saints/gopi.html* which quotes from his book *'Kundalini: Path to*

Higher Consciousness.' The story is quite simple on the surface. Although he had no teacher and was not initiated in any spiritual lineage, he adopted a routine of meditation as part of his mental discipline and practiced concentration exercises for a number of years. In 1937 he had his first Kundalini experience while visualising "an imaginary Lotus in full bloom, radiating light" at the crown of his head.

> Suddenly, with a roar like that of a waterfall, I felt a stream of liquid light entering my brain through the spinal cord. Entirely unprepared for such a development, I was completely taken by surprise; but regaining my self-control, keeping my mind on the point of concentration. The illumination grew brighter and brighter, the roaring louder, I experienced a rocking sensation and then felt myself slipping out of my body, entirely enveloped in a halo of light. It is impossible to describe the experience accurately. I felt the point of consciousness that was myself growing wider surrounded by waves of light. It grew wider and wider, spreading outward while the body, normally the immediate object of its perception, appeared to have receded into the distance until I became entirely unconscious of it. I was now all consciousness without any outline, without any idea of corporeal appendage, without any feeling or sensation coming from the senses, immersed in a sea of light simultaneously conscious and aware at every point, spread out, as it were, in all directions without any barrier or material obstruction. I was no longer myself, or to be more accurate, no longer as I knew

myself to be, a small point of awareness
confined to a body, but instead was a
vast circle of consciousness in which the
body was but a point, bathed in light and
in a state of exultation and happiness
impossible to describe.

I wanted that. In fact, although this had started with the
serious whimsy of giving Margaret the Serpent Fires as part of
her birthday present, I had come to want this sort of experience
badly. Which in itself was probably a huge obstacle to achieving
it.

Y'see before I started all this I had imagined that
awakening the Kundalini might simply be a matter of touching
a couple of psycho-sexual and psycho-spiritual buttons, akin to
licking a nipple while touching a clit at the sime time, or adjusting
the nature sounds on my bedside clock by pressing Mode, Set
and Time simultaneously — that sort of thing. Specific and
almost mechanical techniques which would have specific and
almost predictable results, even if some of the nature sounds
on said clock were a bit wavery. I hoped there might be some
posture, some mantram which might tickle the serpent into
waking so that I can could get on and have fun applying the
god-consciousness. My people awaited me! Return of the King,
and all that.

Even so, Gopi Krishna didn't have too much fun in that
respect. Shortly after the initial awakening, he experienced a
continuous 'luminous glow' around his head and began having
a variety of mental and physical problems. At times he thought
he was going mad, and could find no teacher, no support group
who might advise him.

Every night during sleep I was transported
to a glittering fairyland, where garbed
in luster I glided from place to place,
light as a feather. Scene after scene of
inexpressible glory unfolded before my

vision. The incidents were of the usual
character common to dreams. They
lacked coherence and continuity, but
although strange, fanciful and fantastic,
they possessed a visionary character,
surrounded by landscapes of vastness
and magnificence seldom seen in real
life. In my dreams, I usually experienced
a feeling of security and contentment
with the absence of anything the least
disturbing or disharmonious ...

Ibid

Well, it seems he found the faeries too. I wonder if he lost
his watch? He almost lost his mind. Was I still up for it? Of course.
It was not for Margaret, now, but for the Lost Boy within me who
still wanted to walk the main street of Ashington from the Grand
Corner up to the statue of Jacky Milburn and be like unto a God,
while trying not to hear the folks there muttering as I walked past:
Whae's that twat wi' the shiny face, eh?

I suppose with Margaret gone back to Brussels
for the nonce, the lesson I had to learn here was to do with
working alone. Gopi Krishna managed to arouse the serpent
without the slightest hint of a woman at hand nor even
the faintest throbbing of Tantric Sex. Perhaps his Shakti
was to be found in the prana, as some sources opined,
with both energies just differing aspects of the same thing.

Had anyone else achieved it all on their ownsome? And
was it always as fraught as Gopi Krishna and so many others
have described? Well Freddie Yam had a different take on the
experience, as described at: *realization.org/page/doc0/doc0000.
htm* Before I describe what he did, let me outline what he
experienced.

Suddenly there was light and noise,
brilliant and deafening. One moment
the world was dark, the next a huge jet

of energy, fat and solid as my neck, was emanating at my collar bone and rushing upward in an incandescent torrent, white and frothing like a column of water leaving a hydrant under enormous pressure. It looked like the beam of a floodlight shining up into a clear plastic statue of somebody's neck and head, except the light was boiling and roaring like Niagara Falls. The light, which may have been slightly yellowish ... filled my neck and head completely. It wasn't confined to my spine or anything like a nadi, and, as I said, it originated at the level of my collar bone, not the coccyx.

The noise was huge and real, and the interesting point is that he seemed to be able to see through 360°. He was afraid to move for a while but eventually he stood up and moved around and felt perfectly normal. Except that he wasn't. It soon became apparent to him that he was in an elevated spiritual state.

When I went outside and passed people on the street, they seemed divine to me, especially children. By this I mean that I was aware of their essential goodness and their infinite importance and the casual mundaneness of that infinite importance and the jovial benevolence of the world we all inhabit together. This awareness was so overwhelming that tears of joy came to my eyes. [7]

This condition lasted three days but for him the most striking thing about it was the conviction that the world is not

7. He clearly didn't have to work for the Social Services - *Alan*

only benevolent but also good-humored, almost as if it's a friendly joke that all of us are in on; all of us should be winking at each other. But more than that — far more than that — the experience was profound and beautiful and important. To Freddie it was what people meant when they talked of God; it was love. And for three days it was tangible to him, to the point that he kept crying tears of joy intermittently. "But why shouldn't they?" he noted. "I loved them, not in a soppy way, but as if we were such old friends that we didn't have to bother saying hello."

After three days, the spiritual awareness subsided, although "an attenuated trace of it remains to this day, and I'm extremely grateful for it." His final comment on the experience was simply:

> I am an ordinary person, no better or worse than anybody else. But this experience was a taste of sainthood. If you stayed permanently in this state which I merely visited for three days, you would be a saint. And so I conclude that yoga is a technology for turning people into saints. Should this be a surprise? Indian scriptures have said so for several thousand years.

Did I want to be a Saint though? I wanted that when I was a boy, briefly, as I mentioned earlier. Since then I have wanted to be a good writer and a good husband and a good dad and a down-and-simple good man ... but Saint? I think I might have been Saint Ywi in a previous life on Lindisfarne, but that's another story, and here in the 21st Century I like the pleasures of life too much: A Saturday morning in a nice café somewhere, reading the football news; long walks in the country with my lovely woman; strong tea and dippy-in custard creams; sex and loving kindness with some dirty talk thrown in.

I think I was a bit frightened here. Freddie Yam's technique is so simple, and his initial experiences had so much in common with some of the things I had felt when practising raja yogic techniques in my mid-teens, that I was convinced this would work. I wasn't sure if I was ready for it. I wanted Margaret around. Not to hold my hand and talk me through it, but just so she could phone in sick for me at work the next day, if it all went haywire. "Hello, is that the Centre? Alan won't be in today, he's got a kundalini stuck in his vissudhi and it's causing all sorts of problems. Might be a little difficult getting a sick note from the doctor though …"

It was the simplicity which was so daunting. All he wrote was: "Waking the Kundalini is simple. Just move the prana down and the apana up until they meet and combine." I didn't know what 'apana' was but then neither did he at first. Google knew however: it found 27,500 references under 'prana and apana' in 0.25 seconds. So that was all I had to do then: move the prana down and apana up and my godhood was a cert.

Look I'll make a deal. If all the other techniques fail then at the end of this project I'll give Freddie Yam's technique the best of goes and let you know what happens. Meanwhile try it yourself if you want, but read the warnings very, very carefully.

So what else could I try during these next few weeks *sans* my Shakti? I didn't want to just tread water in the spiritual sense, and I was still wrestling mightily with my French verbs at another level. In fact I could say with great fluency and some understanding: *Si tu savait a quelle point je t'aime. Je t'aime tellement* … If you only knew how much I love you. I love you so much … Of course she had taught me that herself, and no doubt had said it often to any number of her knuckle-dragging microcephalitic Euro-lovers, but it still had a certain incantatory quality for me which, in her absence, evoked her essential otherness − even if she was born and bred in Gosport.

Of course there was plenty of help out there if I wanted to study some 'autosexual tantra,' but it wasn't appealing. There's only so many tissues a man can go through in his lifetime. Okay

I know Philip Larkin's comment: "Sex is far too good to share with anyone else," but I'd had enough of being alone, and mastering lonely techniques. Still, if you want to try for yourself type the word autosex into Google. At that time I got 58,900 hits, while autosex tantra produced 26,700, and every site listed on the first page was German. On the other hand — no pun intended — 'magical masturbation' gave 115 results, and there was a lively, insightful piece at *grant-morrison.com/pop_magic_part_one.htm* which might repay some study, especially if you're into what he uncompromisingly calls the 'Wank Technique'![8]

Sitting here at the PC in my little flat in Wiltshire, what had I achieved so far? Reviewing the bullet points given earlier, if I had to pick out two with any certainty they would be:

"Enlightenment experiences: direct knowing of a more expansive reality." I think that could be found in those trans-dimensional experiences of the empty school room, and Solsbury Hill.

"Exquisite awareness of one's environment (including 'vibes' from others)" and I think this was crystallised on the beach at Hayle, in Cornwall.

What about: "past-life memories; astral travel; direct awareness of auras and chakras; contact with spirit guides through inner voices, dreams or visions; healing powers"?

Well I'd always had fragments of what might be past-life memories, had been out of my body several times, and was certainly getting intense dreams and coy visions. As for the aura and chakras I do actually think I was able to engage with these too, and Margaret had certain experiences of her own as regards possible healing powers that might have been stimulated within me.

So I was getting somewhere, I felt, even if it wasn't particularly serpentine, or cosmically orgasmic. What I had realised though is the experience that is summed up neatly at *swamij.com/shakti.htm* under the title 'The Kundalini Shakti'

8. And you might also try *worldwidewank.com/onanism.html* for Mark Twain's delightful essay in which he cries 'Give me masturbation or give me death!'

where it is stated simply: "There is only one energy: One of the major insights of Tantra and Yoga meditation, possibly the key to the whole science of Tantra, is that there is only one energy in the whole of the universe, and our task is to know that, in direct experience." The writer, Swami Jnaneshvara Bharati, takes us through the concepts step by step, showing that there is one energy (Shakti) in the universe that also keeps changing forms. Each time that energy changes form, we give it a new name. Work through this and don't be put off by the apparent denseness of the terminology. The terms are unfamiliar but bear with them as we don't have too many equivalents in English. Thus:

- Shakti: The universal energy of consciousness is called Shakti
- Kundalini-shakti: The word kunda means a bowl in which fire is burned. Thus, when Shakti resides in a bowl called kunda at the base of the spine, it is called Kundalini-shakti. … Imagine that you are holding a bowl called kunda in your hand. When you plunge the bowl into the river, you say, "I have put the bowl into the river." However, the moment you pull your hand and the bowl out of the river, you say, "I have water in the bowl." In that moment, the river was given a new name, changing it from river to water
- Kundalini: Then, in our language, the word Shakti is dropped away, and the energy in the bowl is simply called Kundalini. In effect, Kundalini-shakti has been given a new name, simply Kundalini. Even though it is now called simply Kundalini, it remains none other than pure Shakti. The only difference, if you can call it a difference, is that the Shakti is now in the bowl
- Prana: A tiny amount of the energy called

Kundalini radiates off of its subtle mass, like steam rising from a bowl of boiling water. That radiating energy is called Prana. Again, once it changes form slightly, it gets a new name. Just like the water turning to steam, while still remaining water, the Kundalini, which is still Shakti, "becomes" Prana

- Nadis: That Prana tends to flow in certain patterns, or lines, like the steam rising in more or less predictable channels. These lines, patterns, or channels are called Nadis. Once again, a new name is introduced

- Chakras, marmas: The thousands of Nadis, with their Prana (that is really both a small amount of Kundalini, and still Shakti), crisscross here and there like minor or major highway intersections. Those major highway intersections are called Chakras (minor intersections are Marmas or Marmashtanas). It is because of this crossing pattern, like highway intersections, or spokes on a wheel, that the word chakra is used, which literally translates as wheel

- Vayus: From there the Chakras, with their different shapes and styles of intersection, cause five flows of energy called Vayus

- Bhutas, tattvas: These take on the qualities of earth, water, fire, air, and space, which are called Tattvas and Bhutas at their subtle and gross levels

- Brain, body, breath: These in turn become the various aspects of our physical brain, body, and breath. Still, they are none other than the Shakti, Kundalini-shakti, Kundalini, and Prana flowing in Nadis, that they were all along.

He makes it all sound very simple, once you've grasped

how one thing flows into another, and they're all the same in the end anyway. Perhaps it is that simple. I stumbled upon a line in my notes which I deemed important enough at the time to keep, but for which I've since lost the reference. It reads: "All unifying, all registering energy field ... what used to be called the ether is now called the neutrino sea or the mnemonic field." Anyone out there find it? Google couldn't. But it seems to be the same thing. In fact, as I experience the work and research this, everything seems to curl back upon itself like the worm Ouroboros – the serpent swallowing its own tail. So let me get this in sequence, coiling and uncoiling my thoughts in the serpentine way, snaking my way across the ground toward gnosis:

Everything is Shakti. Margaret is Shakti. Shakti is Margaret. Margaret is everything. Everything is Margaret. I fuck Margaret. I fuck everything. Everything fucks me. The whole world, the universe is one cosmic fuck. Yeah, I get it now. Even if it does sound like one of the stream-of-consciousness ravings that you could get away with in the early 70s, along with the sideburns and those appalling huge flared trousers we called Loons.

Still an' all, I wish she was back from Brussels, coz the thing we have to try next is ... sex magick!

Chapter 7

The sexual rites found in tantra yoga, Taoist sexual alchemy, karezza, neo-tantra et al form the basis for orthodox religious worship services and are also at the core of the personal spiritual paths of countless individuals. This has been true for millennia and continues to be the case to this day, despite the persecution of sexuality in most modern civilizations. In my opinion, the reason that such strikingly similar sexual rituals have arisen spontaneously in different eras and places — and the reason they so easily cross socio-cultural boundaries — is that sex worship itself is rooted in the neurological hard-wiring of the human body; because it is something which, when practiced correctly, allows the participants to experience what seems to be — what IS, for all intents and purposes — the presence of deity in the person of the sex partner.
www.luckymojo.com/tktantradefinition.
html

I got the above from typing "sex magick definition" into Google, and it also gave a link to the excellent essay by Catherine Yronwode called: 'The Biological Basis of Sacred Sex' at *luckymojo.com/tkbiologicalbasis.html*. I liked her stuff, and have quoted her before. Google picks her up so easily she must be spot-on.

Anyway, she had first read about tantric-style sex (under

the name karezza) in 1962, but it was not until 1975 that she met someone who wanted to try it, although neither of them had a teacher. "It worked for us!" she exulted, "That's all I can say. It worked!" It didn't make them life-partners and it didn't turn either of them into swinging singles, and neither did they join a religious cult. But it did take them to spiritual vistas of sexual beauty and unity. She also came to realise that all of the religious mumbo-jumbo she had read about tantra was just a bunch of socio-cultural veneer laid over a basic biological-spiritual truth: that we have a kind of neurological hard-wiring that we can utilise by developing something akin to the practice of biofeedback training — call it tantra or karezz — that is sort of like learning to 'wiggle your ears' as she puts it. It's something you have to work at, because the volitional control of the musculature involved is not part of our usual training in life.

If you want learn more of what they did, and how, go to those web pages and find out how to surf on the wave of the orgasm without letting the wave break, and how to do the same to your partner while wiggling both your ways into another level of reality.

It was fascinating, but not what I wanted. I wanted a simple magick button which would fling me into a state of gratuitous grace, without much effort but with lots of warmth. And when I looked at the article again I realised that Margaret and I have already been flung into areas of 'sexual beauty and unity', and we had also had so much damned fun. Neither of us had laughed so much in our sex lives; neither of us had had so much sex. What I wanted, and wanted for both of us, was what I might call loving-kindness-fun, and hoped to find some means that would enchant the serpent and all its powers by laughter as much as technique.

Does the kundalini have a sense of humour? Does the Shakti? Well, it's an old occult belief that the Big Bang was as much the creator-god's first cosmic laugh as anything else. And while we're on the topic, remember that ancient Egyptian belief which held that the universe was created by the god Atum masturbating it into existence. So from their point of view the Big Bang, the First Word, the Tetragrammaton, was not so much a divine chortle as a gasping cum. Can you combine them both?

I had had a powerful dream on the last night Margaret was with me, and naturally I put this down to the burgeoning effects of working with her toward the Kundalini. Of course it could equally have been caused by the sheer comfort of the new mattress-topper we had bought from Ikea, but that's hardly productive for the present purpose is it? I mean, Gopi Krishna didn't get where he did by the sort of subdued consumer ecstacies which gave us so much pleasure together, and I'm sure the experience of buying haddock, chips and peas in the Ikea café for a mere pound sterling wouldn't have started a light pulsing in his spirit as it did mine. But this which came to me in the night was something of another Big Dream, so it wasn't the usual stuff I get about wandering around naked in the high street from the waist down, or being alone and unloved in America, or flying in public and helping others to do the same. I had to take it seriously.

In the dream me and Margaret were being shown around a large stately home by its lady owner, who looked and spoke a bit like the actress Maggie Smith in *The Prime of Miss Jean Brodie*. Margaret was somehow involved in trying to track down her ancestors (her family were once very big in Kent, and even have a Quarter named after them), and she talked animatedly to the owner as I dawdled along a little distance behind. After going through the ancient Great Hall the pair of them turned into the private chapel and called me. My dream-mind was on other things and none of them serious, I stepped inside and saw (as if in greyscale but luminous, deep and rich) the huge windows, the sense of a knobby-ended cross rearing up like a snake, a kaleidoscope of light and imagery and grey stone and wood and sanctity and Light searing through me and filling me with such bliss, such a sense of *At last!* that I leaned back against the door frame and wept, copiously. "Are you quite alright?" the lady asked. "Yes" I said, for despite the tears I was in a strange sense laughing also, coz I couldn't have been more alright, couldn't have found greater than this 'perfect peace profound,' this pulse of ecstasy.

Well that was my dream, and it was a good one. Even though the sense of bliss I experienced occurred at dream-level, it was just as valid as any waking emotion because it still hung around me the next day, and I can summon up something of its frisson even now. Whether there was any 'meaning' to the dream or not is probably beside the point. When I asked Margaret if it might have a meaning (and she really is very good at this sort of thing, though I don't necessarily believe it), she put on her coat of many colours, muttered something about seven good years and Donny Osmond as pharoah, and went out make me a nice cuppa tea.

Fascinating though this might be to me, I do accept that unless your name is Carl Gustav Jung and you're milking rich women in the name of enlightenment, other peoples' dreams must be as dreadful to those inflicted by them as those moments in an old peoples' home when the residents get their little jars out and shake the kidney stones inside them. And I bet Freddie Yam and Gopi Krishna never worked in one of those places either.

So what I wanted to find now was something that I could do by myself, until Margaret returned from the Evil Empire. I mean, I didn't want to do anything weird on the self-ecstacy front, like tying myself up before I did the breathing exercises. I can be quite prudish at times in that respect. I knew that somewhere along the Google-line I would eventually dive head first into the realms of the late and great Aleister Crowley; but I wanted my Shakti around in person for when his spirit was summoned up from cyber-space. Until then I hoped to work toward a straightforward, healthy summoning/stumulation of the serpent. And somehow, guided by my Web Angel perhaps, I managed to stumble into Edgar Cayce.

You can't get healthier than Edgar Cayce. He was born on a farm near Hopkinsville, Kentucky in 1877. At the age of six, he told his parents that he could see and talk with 'visions,' sometimes of relatives who had recently died, and even angels. He could also sleep with his head on his schoolbooks and awake with a photographic recall of their contents, even sighting the page upon which the answer appeared. Right from the start he was a bit different. Then at the age of 24 he stumbled upon a talent for psychism that astounded the world, going into areas of prophecy and healing – particularly healing – that changed lives. The countless requests for healing were invariably received through the mail, as the recipients of the readings were usually hundreds of miles away. All he needed was the full name of the person, his address, and where he would be at the appointed time of the reading.

Lying on the couch with his necktie and shoelaces loosened, for better circulation, it was said, he could answer any question put to him. His wife, Gertrude, usually made the suggestions and asked the questions, while his lifelong secretary, Gladys Davis, took everything down in shorthand. After a while, the sleeping Cayce would start to mumble, as though searching for something. Then he would clear his throat and speak in a firm, authoritative voice. "Yes, we have the body," and then go into a half-hour discussion of the physical condition of the person who was ill. Although he was uneducated and untutored, the advice given was staggeringly apt, and the cures he helped effect were widely attested.

There was not a whiff of scandal attached, not a hint of fraud arising from the activities of the 'sleeping prophet' as he became known. The huge publicity did not affect him and neither was he swayed by the offers of fame and large sums of money. Although he never earned more than a modest living at best, he turned down all efforts by others to commercialise on the readings. Desperately poor at times, he once flatly refused an offer of $1,000 a day to go on the stage. A very simple, down-home countryman in his tastes, he was an expert fisherman and a horrible golfer. Look him up at the site given on the next page and marvel that people like him really did and do exist.

The point and relevance of Cayce with regard to my own quest for the Serpent Fires, and my delving into the concept and experience of the Shakti, is that eventually, somebody thought to ask the sleeping Cayce where he was getting his information. He gave two sources his mind apparently succeeded in tapping. One was the unconscious or subconscious mind of the subject himself; the other was what was called the universal memory of nature, Jung's Collective Unconscious, or the Akashic Records. This is the 'Recording Angel', or the 'Book of Life.'

The writer, Kevin Williams, goes on to comment:

> Cayce's mind was able to tap the mass of knowledge possessed by millions of other subconscious minds, including those who have passed over to the spiritual, cosmic realms in death. This would be an almost unlimited source of wisdom, since it was universal and Cayce was unhindered by time and space. Upon this 'Akashic record' is supposedly registered every sound, every thought, every vibration since the beginning of time. Cayce, then was no 'medium.' When this idea first appeared in a reading, few, including Cayce, could believe it. Science knew nothing of any such etheric substance.
>
> *near-death.com/experiences/cayce02.html*

In fact I had stumbled upon Cayce because of J. Van Auken whose pieces have mentioned earlier, and whose 'Kundalini Meditation' appeared on the Association for Research and Enlightenment website. The A.R.E. as it is known, has carried on promulgating Cayce's teachings since his death in 1945, and has an air about its pages that are as straightforward and helpful as the man itself had seemed to be. If you want to look them up then: *edgarcayce.org/ps2/edgar_cayce_story.html* will take you to them.

Getting distracted by the genial air about the man's

photo I think I immediately made the Kentucky Seer into one of my heroes even if his predictions about the forthcoming earth changes make for depressing reading, summarised by Larry A. Wright at *wrightworld.net/edgar.htm*. Mind you, I was a bit taken aback by his love of golf, but only because (many years ago) I had taken a holy vow before my gods never to touch a golf bat, and insisted that my daughters put on my headstone the One Truth I stand by: *All golfers are emotionally malformed* — but I can't be too po-faced in these matters I suppose.

As I read about Cayce (pronounced kay-see just as Crowley rhymes with holy) I felt that yet again things were spiralling back into one another … Cayce/Blavatsky/Akasha - we are all parts of one whole, aspects of one fuck. Maybe on the macrocosmic Great Body of God, me and my experiences are no more than a nipple rising hard with desire?

At any rate J. Van Auken's exercise, as received from the teachings of the entranced Edgar Cayce were those I felt most appropriate for my solo work necessary until Margaret re-appeared. He called this technique 'The Rising Incantation' which is taken from an ancient Egyptian mystical practice as described in Cayce's readings. His words.

> Breathe in deeply, then as you very slowly exhale, direct your consciousness to the lowest chakra and begin moving the life force upward as you chant in a crone "ah ah ah ah ah, a a a a a, e e e e e, i i i i i, o o o o o, u u u u u, m m m m m." Each sound is associated with a chakra. "Ah," with the root chakra (reading 2072-10, "this is not R, but Ah," as the "a" in spa). "A," with the lyden center (sounds like long "a" in able). "E," with the solar plexus (sounds like long "e" in eve). "I," with the heart (a long "i", as in high). "O," with the throat (long "o" as in open).

124

"U," with the pineal (sounds like the
"u" in true). And, "M," with the third
eye (like humming the "m" in room).

edgarcayce.org/ps2/kundalini_meditation_J_Van_
Auken.html

Mr. Auken reminds us that true incanting is an inner sounding which vibrates, stimulates and lifts the life force. He asserts that it is done in a droning manner, with a monotonous, humming tone — vibrating the vocal chords and then directing this vibration to the chakras, thus vibrating them in turn. To me this is reminiscent of the medieval 'wizards that peep and mutter' – intoning their magick words with lips closed and going for the deepest vibration up and down their bodies. Try it yourself with a shopping list. I'm serious. One of the great Eastern gurus (so great that I've forgotten his name) insisted that even nonsense words can be as effective in bringing you to enlightenment as the most revered mantra. Do it in the car on your way to Tescos. It really does get you buzzing.

Van Auken does warn however, that at the final point in the meditation when the crown chakra is being stimulated, the head will be drawn back and the forehead and crown may have pronounced sensations or vibrations. "At the same time the upper body and head may be moving back and forth, or side to side, or in a circular motion (circular is preferable)." I was reminded of Stevie Wonder, his upper body swaying and gyrating as I saw him do when he sang. "These are all natural results of the practice," the writer insists, "and are identified as such in the readings. In the Revelation, St. John associates body-shaking (earthquakes) with the opening of the sixth chakra, followed by 'silence in heaven' as the seventh chakra opens."

Silence in heaven sounded good. I went there once during a near-death experience, going down the classic tunnel and into a realm of whiteness and silence. It certainly wasn't the bland and childish cloud-heaven of Christian belief: this was a clearly defined landscape with distant and very odd dwellings, hills, trees, and all expressed in this 'whiteness' that to me was the utmost in purity and simplicty. There was no sign of any people but a silence and stillness that held consciousness in itself. And then I came back.

So I was ready for the silence in heaven experience. And it went like this …

As I sat in a reasonably meditative posture in the silence of my sitting room, facing south, I used Van Auken's previous technique to get me in tune. And then I began the intonations, always hoping that the people in the flat above me wouldn't hear and perhaps register them as death-rattles, rather than sacred sonics. I'm not being crass again. In a crowded world and a busy life, you have to pay attention to such detail or you get like the magus 'Frater Achad' (Google him for details), who had such a burst of illumination that he cried out "I have stripped away the veils of illusion!" and matched it by stripping off his clothes. Which was fine and inoffensive in itself, and an entirely apposite act, only he was on the main street in Vancouver at the time and so got arrested and jailed for indecent exposure.

In that respect I didn't want the woman upstairs getting an ambulance for me, and me having to explain to the paramedics. I had been brought up, magickally speaking, to accept Eliphas Levi's dictum that the magician should 'Know, Will, Dare — above all, Be Silent,' so it was hard for me to blabber about such activities.

But I sat nicely and I tried the different tones and made the mistake (I think it was a mistake) of starting the lowest *ah* in the key of *doh*, and then going upward to a falsetto *m* in the key of *tee*. No vibratory response at all, except an anxiety to hit the right notes.

So I started again and kept the same deep tone for each, trying to keep each one like a Tibetan singing bowl, but it only began to get a response when I touched each chakra with my left hand. Though to be honest it was only a partial response. That is to say the chakras below my heart did nothing, while those from my heart up did resonate like tuning forks.

Spiritually, am I dead from the heart down? Did I need my Shakti to give me a boost, to create a synergistic flow of energies? I think I did. As I thought about that the old song 'Three Wheels on my Wagon' floated into my head and that was about right: you could still get along on three wheels, but not far and not fast, and not without causing damage to rest of the wagon.

Mind you the great mystics and magicians affirm that we are never alone. Some of them will say that we are surrounded by Masters, like HPB with those dodgy characters shown earlier. Others will insist upon the ever-present nature of our Guides, and others still about the all-enveloping concerns of the loving dead. Part of the Kundalini experience is supposed to lead onto: '... extrasensory perception; out-of-body experiences; past-life memories; astral travel; direct awareness of auras and chakras; contact with spirit guides through inner voices, dreams or visions ...'

So was I making contact with spirit guides in any way shape or form? Did the genteel charming of my inner snake have any knock-on effects in this direction?

I thought about the time not long before when I had visited Margaret in London. Her company had booked her in to stay overnight at the Savoy, where George Gershwin had once played the piano, Noel Coward sang, Fred Astaire danced, and Keith Moon urinated in the fireplace. Of course when she was in the shower I read all the brochures left lying about, hid them, and impressed her with my vast knowledge of the place when we explored it later.

"How do you know all that?" she asked, dead impressed, all soft and lovely and doe-eyed and dopey.

"Ah," I said, giving her an inscrutable look, "we Serpent Kings have our own forms of knowledge. We can plug into the akashic records, y'know."

"What's wrong with your eyebrows?" she asked, making them level again and plucking the hairs where they join in the middle, as witches eyebrows are said to do.

That night we dined with someone I felt I had known in a previous life, which stirred up lively things in my psyche. And then on the personal level Margaret and I had a sort of spat back in our room. Or a little misunderstanding. Normally we handle these things very well, being mature adults, and I've developed a strategy whereby as soon as she can admit it's all her fault, then we can move on quickly enough and have fun again. But for some reason she wouldn't do this,[9] and I hardly slept that night.

While she went to work the next day I was in a state of some distress, as I have a tendency to turn everything into an end of the world scenario. I took a tube (into the underworld, see?) to Paddington, intending to go back home and have a bout of deep mystical introspection that unenlightened souls might confuse with a right sulk. Pausing only to grab the freebies being offered at the station concourse by some tosser called Loyd Grossman, and shoving six of his trial size jars of tomato and chilli pasta sauce into my bag, I had instead the irresistible compulsion to go on a sort of frantic hither and thither Power Walk around parts of London that were completely unknown to me.

It was misty, light rain, cold. I felt troubled and ill. My mind was racing and so were my legs. My insides were churning, and this was nothing to do with the overpriced and under cooked bacon butty I got from Le Comte de St Germaine in Burger King. I didn't want to lose her, see? She was gold, she was goodness, a grail among gals, and I felt I'd made a prick of myself over the canapés.

Take note all you chelas, coz this is important: even mighty adepts like me can get as confused by human loving as anyone who is just rising from the primordial slime of puberty. Cosmic wisdom doesn't necessarily bring earthly maturity. As Crowley or someone of that ilk once said: 'The planes are separate.' Just look at the cock-ups he'd made with his life — and him being the Logos of the Aeon an' all.

So I didn't know where the hell I was — and I use that phrase deliberately. It was only when the urge to walk stopped as suddenly as it started that I had a vague sense of familiarity.

---

9. *I've never done this* - Margaret

It wasn't so much the architecture as the street names. And I realised with a shock that I was only yards away from 3 Queensborough Terrace, the location of which I had studied on various street maps when writing *Priestess – the Life and Magic of Dion Fortune,* yet had never visited coz they only gave me a £200 advance, which was risible even then given the amount of research that was needed. But – whingeing apart - for a long time this had been her home. This had contained her specialist temples. It was from this place that she had developed a Western Tantra, and expanded the Mysteries of Atlantis, Egypt and Celtic Britain, and where she had raised the spirits of Merlin and the Pendragon when this land was in dire peril of Nazi invasion. This, in a sense, was my alma mater, and I spent a little while honouring it accordingly, even if it was now just a block of flats with junk mail on the doorstep.

I still had to walk, but more calmly. I went to nearby Kensington Park, which looked lovely, and sat on a bench next to the Serpentine and drank in the sun which had suddenly emerged. I imagined the light from the sun as it came across the water soaking into me with each in-breath, and tried to feel my aura being purified, and I remembered when I first met Margaret again after many years, on the old pack-horse bridge in Bradford on Avon, and the sun shone upon her face and took my breath away in an instant, and she was young and cheeky, golden and shining, and my heart was carried off down rivers of windfall light, and I knew that she was The One. And then, circling back in my thoughts, I tried not to think of me having made a tit of myself the night before.

Not far away, next to this stretch of water further along in Hyde Park, Helena Blavatsky had first met her Master on a moonlit night in 1861. Oh but I could have done with some ascended being to come along just then and tell me things. I needed some wisdom. A fella strolled past who was the spitting image of Jack Palance, but that wasn't much help. Another walked by who looked like a young version of Swami Lakshmanjoo, but the lamb kebab gave it away. I could have done with a Master then: someone who would reveal the future, and tell me what to do, and absolve me of all responsibility and decision-making. I wondered if the Swami had ever made a tit of himself. I doubted it: his pictures seemed filled with grace. On the other hand, he wouldn't have had a Shakti like mine. I felt I had far more to lose than he would ever have known..

At my feet, on the water's edge, swans and ugly crows were after my deep-fill Tesco sandwiches but they had no chance. Swans mated for life, I told myself, and I was jealous of them; and crows were my totem birds, who gain life from dead things. Then, as I did pranayamic things with my own self-pitying miseries, sucking them in and out, I had the sudden sense that Dion occupied the bench with me, on my right hand side. Although to be precise, it wasn't Dion Fortune so much as her earthly self known as Violet Firth.

"Hello Violet," I said out loud, coz there was no-one else around to think me insane, and it seemed to enforce the presence. So before I go into the rest of the encounter, I think I'd better Google her up and get her across in some detail for all those who — shame upon them! — have never heard of her…

> Very little is known of her early life except that she is reputed to have had visions of 'Atlantis' when she was four and later in her life she believed that she had been a temple priestess there. During puberty she is said to have developed mediumistic abilities. In 1906 she joined the Theosophical movement when her family moved to London but did not find their ideas inspiring. When she was twenty Dion worked under a woman who had travelled to India and studied occult techniques which Dion claimed she used against her in the form of 'Psychic Attacks'. Dion fought off these attacks suffering a nervous breakdown in the process. By the age of twenty-three she was a lay psychoanalyst having studied psychology

but felt that neither Carl G. Jung or Sigmund Freud really understood the complexity and ability of the mind. During the end of World War I she met and worked with Irishman, the occultist and freemason, Theodore Moriarty which led to her write her well known book 'Psychic Self-Defence' which is seen as her magical autobiography.

Well, it was me who actually wrote that about *Psychic Self Defence* being a curious sort of life story — or as much of a life story as she was willing to reveal. It's a classic. Go and buy it. They went on:

> Fortune was initiated into an outer order of the Hermetic Order of the Golden Dawn known as the London Temple of the Alpha and Omega Lodge of the Stella Matutina in 1919, but she formed her own order known as the 'Fraternity of the Inner Light' which was based upon esoteric Christianity, originally part of the Golden Dawn but eventually forming itself as an independent after Moina Mathers (one of the founders of the Golden Dawn) asked Dion to leave.
>
> During the winter of 1923/24 Dion then spent time in Glastonbury which became a place she would retreat to regularly involving her own thoughts in the Celtic Otherworld she claimed lay beneath the Tor. During this time she claimed to have been in spiritual contact with the Greek philosopher Socrates, the nineteenth-century Chancellor of England Lord Erksine, and later the great Arthurian magus himself 'Merlin.' She wrote many of her experiences down in the book 'Glastonbury: Avalon of the Heart.'

Fortune married Thomas Penry Evans in 1927. He became nicknamed Merlin/Merl by many of Fortune's followers. Unfortunately he divorced her in 1939 after many reputed arguments, he re-married later.

Fortune also formed a pilgrim centre known as the 'Chalice Orchard Club' whilst in Glastonbury, along with a temple dedicated to the 'Mysteries of Isis' in West London known as the 'Belfry.' During her life, and since, she has received a large following. Many of her books are still read by occultists/neo-Pagans. Just after the World War II she was struck down with leukaemia and died at the age of 54.

mystical-www.co.uk/glastonbury/dionf.htn

Well that's the bland version from the Mystical World Wide Web, and they've done a decent enough job even if the cheeky sods have stolen lots of it from my own book Now sit back, put your Googles aside, and try to take on board my brief version, as written in *The Old Sod*, my biography of the kabbalist and magician William G. Gray:

> And then there was 'Dion Fortune' (pen-name of Violet Firth), who was Womanhood's answer to Aleister Crowley and the Shakti of the Age. Whatever Crowley did for magick from the masculine point of view, with as much publicity as he could muster, DF as they called her, did very quietly and secretly from the distaff side. She was born in 1890 and died in 1946. She was an initiate in the Hermetic Order of the Golden Dawn and saw it in its zenith, then later formed her own Fraternity of the Inner Light, where they worked the

magic of the West: of Atlantis, Ys and Egypt; of the Celts and Scandinavians; of King Arthur and the Holy Grail, and explored all of those obscure by-ways that might now be termed 'Native British.' Although there was a Christian Mystic section for the less able, she specialised in the magic of the Great Goddess figures. Her main temple was at 3 Queensborough Terrace in London, but she also had a small centre right at the foot of Glastonbury Tor. Her books such as *The Mystical Qabalah, Applied Magic,* and the very odd *Psychic Self-defence* have been much copied but never surpassed. Her novels *The Sea Priestess* and *Moon Magic* are utterly beautiful in their prose and almost hypnotic in their magical effect upon the reader. Most witches, crafting their art in the early days after the war, stole ideas and attitudes from her writing; every magician owes her a debt for the sheer clarity of exposition on obscure Hermetic topics they might never have grasped otherwise. Every woman who has ever challenged the patriarchy of modern times should give her no small degree of gratitude for paving the way.

There. You won't find that on the Web, and *The Old Sod* is Out of Print now, and some idiot on E-bay is offering his copy for $1,000. Anyone remotely tempted to pay such a ridiculous sum is encouraged to contact me immediately.

So here we are in Kensington Gardens, 260 acres of parkland in the heart of London. I had never been there before, and was unaware of the bronze statue of Peter Pan, or the Diana, Princess of Wales Memorial Playground and seven-mile Memorial Walk, or even the Elfin Oak which is, apparently, a partially hollow stump, carved with the figures of faeries, elves and various small animals following the contours of the wood. If I hadn't been in such a strop and feeling sorry for myself, I might have tried to track these down. As it was I found myself alone on a bench communing in a gentle way with a woman who had died 60 years before.

"Hello Violet," I said, but there was no answer in words, no inner voice as is supposed to happen as part of the Kundalini experience. And yet … commune we did. It's very hard to describe. Listen, try to remember (or more realistically try to imagine) what it was like when you were a child lying in bed at night, and your Mam came in to look at you, to see if you were alright. Neither of you said anything, but that silent sense of two-way contact was profound and memorable, as any parent can confirm.

It was a bit like that then. Not that Violet was giving me any warm parental *there-there-there* comfort during my self-induced emotional torment. Far from it, she was desperately unhappy herself, I felt, and I seem to have picked up the time when her own marriage was breaking up and she would come to this quiet place to quietly fall apart and wonder what the fuck she was going to do next.

"You'll get through it Violet," said I, her first biographer. "You'll set the world alight. You are loved by people yet unborn. I love you."

I think she might have had some comfort from that, because she went as suddenly as she came and I was left with the light rippling on the water, and the swans and crows.

So what actually happened there? Let's discount pure imagination: I'm smart, me! I can tell the difference. Then did I actually touch upon the living essence of Violet Firth during a bleak time in her life when her marriage was crumbling? Was I, to her perceptions, a sombre spirit from the future giving her succor? Maybe it was to do with what Mystress Angelique Serpent mentioned earlier, touching on the DNA: "The double helix we're unfolding here is a hologram that is reflected in every single cell of your body. That's the power of Kundalini inside of you, awake, and dancing." She had had memories of being her grandfather, when he was an officer: perhaps if DF was part of my spiritual DNA, I was having memories of her when she was in wars of another kind. Or did my own distress activate a kind of projection from my unconscious, using the image of Dion Fortune to give it shape so that I was communing with my own angst?

I don't know and to be honest I don't care. Quite simply, on a park bench in London, at the end of a beam of light, something happened that moved me deeply. And if, when you try to Google your own serpents into awareness using some or all or none of the techniques I've given here, you get strong dreams, hypnogogic visions, past life memories, awareness of auras and chakras, and a sense of contact with spirit guides then let them happen. Indulge and marvel and worry about your sanity another time, coz it's a short life. But don't ever, ever buy that tomato and chilli pasta sauce from Loyd Grossman.

Chapter 8

There is no Grace
There is no guilt
This is the Law
Do what thou Wilt
              Aleister Crowley, on becoming
                    Logos of the Aeon

Whey lads an' lasses,
Aah   divvn't   knaa
much aboot Politics,
but Aah'll dae me
best.
        George Grant, on being elected
    Labour MP for Ashington, c1970

When I was 14 I had a huge dilemma. As I walked forlornly along the dog-shit wastes of the grandly named but treeless Second Avenue, in Ashington, which is set out in a grid-pattern of bleak red brick terraces, I agonised about what career-path I should take. I paced along and then up to the Grand Corner which was then the centre of a tau-cross of roads. To the east was the way to Newbiggin, which was then – to me – a paradisiacal seaside town with golden beaches; to the west was the road to Morpeth, and the lush but empty realms of Northumbria; to the south was the long winding road to Newcastle, which was our Holy City. These were the only three roads out of Ashington because there was nothing to the north but massive pit heaps – the famed Ashington Alps. Mind you some wag once wrote that there was actually a fourth road — that of football. But thanks to my own ineptitude, I never got beyond the position of right drawback in any team I played, so that was never an option.

If I wanted to avoid the pits I needed a fourth road of my own, hence the dilemma I mentioned at the beginning of this book. Did I join the RAF and become a pilot, flying English Electric Lightnings at Mach 2 through what would surely in future be the Mig-haunted skies above Ashington, shooting down the Russkies with my Firestreak air-to-air missiles? or did I become a Boddhisattva, choosing to forgo the eternal bliss of Nirvana in order to be reborn once more and help my fellow man – even if it did mean being nice to Ron the Neck and all those among my peers with the interestingly low brows who were good at games and insufferable to lesser mortals like myself. It was a tough one to call, I felt, but on the whole I favoured divinity and the saffron robes of illumination to the derring-do and bollock-hugging g-suits of the Interceptors. All I had to do now was tell my Mam ...

Honestly, what a pillock I was. Listen, if you're still a young'un and have a chance to do something bold and dashing, but some guru-type tries to suck you toward god-head and explain the meaning of life to you along the way to your bank, choose the outer world every time. Light those the afterburners and go for Mach 1 at least. I'd have been a helluva fighter pilot, me. And the reason I'm not is partly down to Aleister Crowley.

Before Margaret went back to Brussels she looked over what I had written, sitting on the bed with the hard copy on her lap. She wore my red t-shirt, big knickers, thick woolly bed-socks and she was still the sexiest woman on the planet. Me, I was like a schoolboy, eager for his teacher's praise. She leant over the manuscript and her long hair fell forward over the pages, so she couldn't have seen that my face was shining as I watched her.

"But Alan ... why do you always spell magick with a 'k'?"

Now there is the crux of the matter. I was ready for this. I read out the paragraph I had prepared earlier from *alt.magick FAQ*

> Crowley revived the archaic 'ick' spelling that had dropped out of fashion by the early 1800s. 'K' is the eleventh letter of the English alphabet. The number eleven has quite a few symbolical imports. Eleven is the number attributed to the Qlippoth (chaotic, unbalanced forces in the Qabalah). Eleven represents the union of the microcosm (pentagram – five) with the macrocosm (hexagram – six). On a Thelemic note, eleven is the number of words in "Do what thou wilt shall be the whole of the Law," the number of letters in Abrahadabra, and the number attributed to Nuit. 'K' can also be seen as standing for kteis (vagina – cup), the complement to the peos (penis – wand), which directly relates to the creative power of magick and is symbolic of the Great Work. On a more mundane level, the 'k' helps to distinguish magick from stage magic (prestidigitation).
>
> *asiya.org/altmagickfaq/#p1q2*

"Who is Crowley?" she asked and then added, peering over the edge of the bed and down on the floor at me: "And I wish you'd stop feigning tonic clonic seizures when I ask things like this."

Honestly though (and I can say this now she's gone) Honestly! *Who is Aleister Crowley?* she asked! Did my brilliant, wise, beautiful Shakti really say that? In historical terms that's like asking who Winston Churchill was, or Elvis, or Siddharta, or Gandhi, or my Uncle Neville Duke who held the World Air Speed record.

"Crowley was …" I gasped, "Crowley was …"

"The short version Alan, please."

It was Herman Hesse who wrote that no-one hears about Abraxas by accident. And the same is true of Aleister Crowley. I don't know exactly where I was and what I was doing when I first heard of him, but it was in Ashington and probably in one of the newspaper articles reflecting on how he had once been branded the 'Wickedest Man in the World,' and yet was now being rediscovered as one of the most inspiring.

Listen, he had street cred you wouldn't believe. In his youth he had been a world class mountaineer and conquered some of the highest peaks in the Himalayas; he also did much the same on spiritual levels. He summoned angels and demons. He was a chess master, a renowned poet (although much of it hasn't stood the test of time), tireless explorer, hunter, trickster, bully, traitor, novelist, prolific writer of some of the most influential occult books of the 20th Century, socialite, sponger, one of the greatest conversationalists of his generation, libertine, drug addict, and Logos of the Aeon. For those who don't know what a Logos of the Aeon is, then basically it means that the boy Jesus had had his chance, his day. After 1904 and the revelation in Cairo, we should take up the good news of Crowleyanity and start to fuck for heaven. He was the occult world's equivalent of a rock star, 60 years before rock music appeared.

In fact Crowley was to become adored by the gods of Rock: The Beatles put him on the cover of one the most influential albums of all time, *Sergeant Pepper's Lonely Hearts Club Band*, and you can see him peering strongly out from amidst a crowd of other celebrities such as Karl Marx, Mae West, Laurel and Hardy, George Bernard Shaw, Bob Dylan, Oscar Wilde, Lenny Bruce, Carl Gustav Jung, H.G.Wells, the Marquis de Sade, Tony Curtis, Aubrey Beardsley, Dylan Thomas and Marilyn Monroe — and a host of other illuminati.

Then there was Jimmy Page, the demonic little lead guitarist of the apocalyptic rock band Led Zeppelin, who purchased Boleskine, Crowley's old home on the shores of Loch Ness, and became a major collector of his works.

Graham Bond, who founded the Graham Bond Organisation in 1963 with the hugely influential John McLaughlin, the divine Jack Bruce and awesome Ginger Baker, believed that he was Crowley's bastard son, and Bond's music was deeply influenced by Crowley's philosophy.

The Rolling Stones paid their own homage to Crowley, as shown by the album *Their Satanic Majesties Request*, plus their involvement with the avant-garde film director Kenneth Anger, whose tone and projects were pure Crowleyan.

David Bowie, also deeply fascinated by what was then called 'The Occult' mentioned Crowley's magickal Order of The Golden Dawn in his song 'Quicksand' and was very heavily involved in the darker elements of the Crowleyan lifestyle.

While Ozzy Osbourne and the band Black Sabbath owed more than a little to The Master Therion, to give him one of his many names.

Another Heavy Metal band Iron Maiden released an album entitled *Best of the Beast*, with one of the tracks called 'The Number of the Beast.' which referred to Crowley's belief that he was the Beast 666 from the Bible. The punk rock bands of the 1970s also paid their own kinds of rough homage to Crowley and what they fancied were his ideals.

And rock music aside, you couldn't open a novel without him appearing in it as the Prince of Darkness. Martin Booth collected many of these: in Somerset Maugham's early novel, *The Magician*, he was the basis for Oliver Haddo. He also starred as Karswell in M.R. James's *Casting the Runes*; as Oscar Clinton in H. R. Wakefield's *He Cometh and He Passeth By;* as Apuleius Charlton in *A Black Solitude*; as Rowley Thorne in Manly Wade Wellman's *Thorne* stories; as Hugo Astley in Dion Fortune's *The Winged Bull;* as Caradoc Cunningham in Colin Wilson's *Man without a Shadow*; as Dr Trelawney and Scorpio Murtlock in Anthony Powell's *Dance to the Music of Time* sequence of novels; as Mocata in Dennis Wheatley's *The Devil Rides Out*; as Theron Ware in James Bush's *Black Laster;* and as Swaroff in Ethel Archer's *The Hieroglyph,* to name but some.

In 1975 Snoo Wilson wrote a stage play, *The Beast,*

which was put on by the Royal Shakespeare Company: it was revived and rewritten in the 1980s. In 1986, the Ballet Rambert staged a production called *Ceremonies* at Sadler's Wells, based upon rituals Crowley had investigated and upon which he had worked.

Although Crowley's own books hardly attracted many readers in his lifetime you can now find them as mass-market paperbacks, while his *Confessions* has never been out of print in 40 years. Google in "Aleister Crowley" and you get 980,000 hits. There is a nice and simple intro to him at *dracoart.net/crowley/ crowley.html*

> Edward Alexander (Aleister) Crowley …was born October 12, 1875 in Leamington Spa, England. His parents were members of the Plymouth Brethren, a strict fundamentalist Christian sect. As a result, Aleister grew up with a thorough biblical education and an equally thorough disdain of Christianity.
>
> He attended Trinity College at Cambridge University, leaving just before completing his degree. Shortly thereafter he was introduced to George Cecil Jones, who was a member of the Hermetic Order of the Golden Dawn. The Golden Dawn was an occult society led by S.L. MacGregor Mathers which taught magick, qabalah, alchemy, tarot, astrology, and other hermetic subjects. It had many notable members (including A.E. Waite, Dion Fortune, and W.B. Yeats), and its influence on the development of modern western occultism was profound.
>
> Crowley was initiated into the Golden Dawn in 1898, and proceeded to climb up rapidly through the grades. But in 1900 the order was shattered by schism, and Crowley

left England to travel extensively throughout the East. There he learned and practiced the mental and physical disciplines of yoga, supplementing his knowledge of western-style ritual magick with the methods of Oriental mysticism.

In 1903, Crowley married Rose Kelly, and they went to Egypt on their honeymoon. After returning to Cairo in early 1904, Rose (who until this point had shown no interest or familiarity with the occult) began entering trance states and insisting to her husband that the god Horus was trying to contact him. As a test, Crowley took Rose to the Boulak Museum and asked her to point out Horus to him. She passed several well-known images of the god and led Aleister straight to a painted wooden funerary stele from the 26th dynasty, depicting Horus receiving a sacrifice from the deceased, a priest named Ankh-f-n-khonsu. Crowley was especially impressed by the fact that this piece was numbered 666 by the museum, a number with which he had identified since childhood.

The upshot was that he began to listen to Rose, and at her direction, on three successive days beginning April 8, 1904, he entered his chamber at noon and wrote down what he heard dictated from a shadowy presence behind him. The result was the three chapters of verse known as Liber AL vel Legis, or The Book of the Law. This book heralded the dawning of the new aeon of Horus, which would be governed by the Law of Thelema. 'Thelema' is a Greek word meaning 'will,' and the Law of Thelema is often stated as: 'Do what thou wilt.' As the prophet of this new aeon, Crowley spent the rest of his life working to develop and establish Thelemic philosophy.

To his critics at the time (i.e. almost everyone on the planet), the philosophy of Thelema was one of what they charmingly termed 'sexual deviancy' and devil worship. He was as openly bisexual as anyone dared to be then, and Martin Booth, summary of him goes as follows: "… Crowley is still remembered not just for his bisexuality, 'evil' or even his magic, but for the fact that he proposed a philosophy, albeit unworkable and most usually misinterpreted, which sought to raise human dignity in a dehumanised world against which he actively and dedicatedly resisted.

"In short, Crowley was a characteristically unorthodox modern man for a dissenting, questioning modern world. His only trouble was that he was born half a century or so too early." *digital-brilliance.com/kab/essays/magick-life.htm*

In a poll conducted by the BBC in 2002 to find The 100 Greatest Britons, Crowley was voted number 73, just behind King Henry Vth and just before Robert the Bruce.[10] Although his spirit was firmly in my psyche as a lad, he came from a very different world to me, and the man himself would never have been accepted in the two pubs and twenty seven working man's clubs in Ashington coz they'd have written him off as a posh bastard and a bit of a poof. Plus I think he'd have had real problems with the all-powerful Ashington Mams, all of whom were avatars of the Dark Goddess in Her most terrifying and destructive mode. Still an' all, I think he was just The Business, even if I wouldn't have liked him in person.

I could just picture him on the movie screen of my mind:

---

10. To see the rest of them, go to *wordiq.com/definition/100_Greatest_ Britons* and be prepared to quibble.

Int. A Colliery House in Ashington. Day.

The Great Beast makes a grand entrance into the living room, stamping the lino with his silver-tipped cane, tipping his homburg and declaiming to the startled family sitting next to the roaring coal fire:

THE BEAST
Do what thou Wilt shall be the whole of the Law!

THE DAD
Eh?! Whae's that gadgy?

THE MAM
Divvn't stand there taalkin' like that, hinny.
Howway in an' hev a nice cuppa tea.

THE BAIRN
[nervously]
Er … Love is the Law. Aye … Love under Will.

He's an icon, see. Perhaps the greatest icon in magick there will ever be. It doesn't matter if the reality of the icon consists of no more than a few pixels on a screen: once you click on it wondrous things can open up, and all sorts of things start moving before your astonished eyes. He is a gateway to greater

things, even if he did crap on someone's grand piano and leave his visiting card in the turd.

Inspired by him and his poetry, I once tried to invoke Pan on the empty beach at Whitley Bay, although it should have been a woodland to get the full effect. Never mind, I was in love with Siân Bottomley and there was a big moon rising in the sky or it might have been just in my head. I know there was lots of golden sand and a rising tide and the distant ruined priory of Tynemouth Abbey to stride toward, and the teenage feeling of: "I have omnipotence at my command and eternity at my disposal!" as was expressed by the French magus Eliphas Levi, although he never anticipated the sheer beauty of its declamation in Geordie: *Aah hev omni-pohtence at me kermmand, me, an' eetornity at me dispohsill.* But try the *Hymn to Pan* yourself — at least the opening lines.

> Thrill with lissome lust of the light,
> O man! My man!
> Come careering out of the night
> Of Pan! Io Pan!

It starts brilliantly but goes off a bit, has some ups and downs, then perks up again (like life I suppose) and gives that marvellous brace of lines:

> With hoofs of steel I race on the rocks
> Through solstice stubborn to equinox

Io, by the way is the ancient Moon Goddess. You can read the whole evocative poem at *d21c.com/wal9/poems/crowley. html* and chant it at your leisure. After some fierce battles with the energies and faeries in Margaret's strange house in Brussels I did my own mini-rite of Pan using this poem to calm their savage breasts and it seemed to do some good, although the bastards still never returned my watch.

So did Pan come to me on that Northumbrian beach, all cloven-footed and horny? Did the supreme pagan deity possess me, enwrap me in his arms and carry me off? Would he have buggered me, or made mad passionate love to my inner feminine self? Did I have any cosmic experience other than sand in my shoes and a drug-free delight?

Well … no. Nothing overtly astonishing happened. But I think from that moment I became weaned away from my Judaeo-Christian heritage and more in tune with that notion of Spirit of Place which has come to obsess me.

Try that invocation now. Say it out loud. Say it with passion, because that's what makes the magick. Say it with your partner. Say it in some appropriate place. Think nice things of Crowley but don't ever think that he was a nice man. I know of magicians who have been overshadowed by Crowley to such an extent that they had to psychically banish him. Similar has happened with others re Dion Fortune, the witch 'Robert Cochrane,' William G. Gray and Robbie Williams. It's not necessarily anything to do with spirit possession, I think. Or not always. But we can be so infected by ideas, possibilities, and become so attuned to the originator's mind and soul that we can't get them out of our heads. I believe that we are all parts of one corporate whole, in any case, so that we can become so connected with another soul (even a discarnate one) that we flow into each other. Time doesn't exist, not really. Everything — past/present/future — is happening at once.

Plus I also think that places can also obsess us. How often have we been enchanted with a place so much that we almost pine for it, and constantly imagine or wish that we were there, and try to recreate it with photographs and mementos. And of course the act of being in love with another human is even more intense, and means that your beloved is gonna be in your head and heart in delightful but often exhausting ways, especially if it's not mutual! Then you can know hell on earth.

This is all part of the Cosmic Fuck idea of course. We are part of each other, part of the great cosmic sex act which surges and pulses behind the scenes and below the horizon of our consciousness, and maybe I'm nothing more than something very tiny within the divine sperm cell, looking frantically for the egg. This is Pan — the All. So maybe He came to me on the beach at dusk in Whitley Bay after all, planting a seed of inner fire. Maybe he will come to you too, if you invoke him with passion.

Know that there isn't a magician borne who hasn't wanted to thrill with the lissome lust of the light at some time in his or her Work. I vowed that when Margaret came back we would go to some woodland place and I would declaim this poem/invocation in magnificent and ringing tones, and then we would make love beneath the oaks and summon up ancient lovings.

The importance of Crowley to most of us was that he regarded sex as a sacrament. He practised it right vigorously and (given the dour morality of the time) surprisingly openly with men and women. He explored almost every sexual highway and byway that came to him though he was never a pedophile. And throughout his extraordinary life he persisted in the belief — no, the certainty — that the sexual act could elevate us toward the gods, and help every man and woman to become a Star. Not in the crass Hollywood or nine-day wonder sense of stardom, but as a burst of stellar consciousness and divinity, for in Crowley's cosmology certain vast "stars" (or aggregates of experience) may be described as Gods.

In 1912 he was promoted to the leadership of the English branch of the *Ordo Templi Orientis* and he used this order ever afterwards as a vehicle for popularizing the Law of Thelema, as well as the practice of the Supreme Secret of the O.T.O. During his lifetime, this secret was zealously guarded, although it wasn't hard to fathom the hints given out in the esoteric literature of the day, and also by Crowley himself. However, as Alexander Duncan points out in his neat essay, the Supreme Secret of the O.T.O. was nothing other than the use of sex in the pursuit of spiritual enlightenment — equivalent in fact to a Western Tantra. *religioustolerance.org/thelema3.htm*

And coincidentally or not, Crowley's resurgence and recognition came at the same time the contraceptive pill transformed and set free a whole generation of women. According to the Catholic journal *The Tablet*:

> The advent of the contraceptive pill in the Sixties led to a revolution in sexual behaviour across the Western world. Procreation could now be separated from love-making, and accordingly the emphasis moved from birth prevention to sexual relationships. For the first time in history sexual freedom did not bring fear of unwanted pregnancy, and many took advantage of the opportunities science had won for them. All the Christian Churches were challenged by these developments.
>
> *thetablet.co.uk/cgi-bin/register.cgi/tablet-00296*

Suddenly, there was a whole generation of young women who wanted to indulge in sex without fear, and know things that their mothers and grandmothers could never have known. Taking away the braggadocio of youth there really was an awful lot of sexual activity going on around me in the sin pits of Ashington, in the back rows of the Wallaw, in the alleyway behind the Three Ones Club, in those quiet and frantic hours amid the endless terraces when the youth of the town could persuade their parents to go out for the evening, or boldly on view in the shape of the ithyphallic Maxwell, sitting knees apart on the green bench off Station Bridge, rasping out *Wrrrrrrh! Let's see yah black patch me bonny lass!* to any likely lass who walked past.[11]

Mind you, being almost paralytically shy, I never got owt until I was 18, and then with a great cry of relief which almost split the dawn, and created enough tears of gratitude to fill a coal mine.

11. To see a picture of Maxwell as Sex God go to: *alric.pwp.blueyonder. co.uk/2a.html*

Even so, even for the slow among us, things improved for the boys too. Before what you might call the Crowleyan Consciousness took root a lusty lad couldn't get his todger out without a real risk of going blind and/or plummeting into insanity. Dictionaries still defined masturbation as 'self-abuse' or 'bodily self-pollution.' Yet suddenly, particularly following the 'Trial of Lady Chatterley's Lover' which saw the obscenity laws redefined forever, there was a whole range of books and titillating articles which helped the ordinary working class lad to at least see what It looked like, and words enough to persuade us that It was good. Most of them seemed to be in Maxwell's haversack.

So thank the gods that someone took on the Church, and it does wonders for your spirit to realise that Crowley and his erstwhile band had been challenging the Sterility Cultus of modern Christianity with all the passion they could muster. In a sense it was almost as though his shade looked upon the increasingly sexually adventurous generations and urged them: *Go on, do it* … And if there were any hesitant souls asking in tumescent bewilderment: "Do what, exactly?" Then he would utter the message of Thelema which cried: "Do what thou Wilt shall be the whole of the Law!" To which his followers, or sympathisers, would respond: "Love is the Law: Love under Will."

By all accounts and interpretations (Crowley's own especially) it's not a doctrine of sexual self-indulgence, though to be honest I've never truly fathomed a certain meaning for myself. If you look on the Web there's a bewildering collection of groups and individuals proclaiming their own versions of the Thelemic message. The very first one I Googled at *thelema. org/* (which claimed to be non-profit making) even allows you to download Crowley's seminal text Liber Al vel Legis, or the *Book of the Law*. I don't know if they're any good, but have a look.

I also found *templex.org* where you can learn about the three degrees of Western Ceremonial Sex Magick, namely:

Alphaism

Magickal Abstention.

Not allowing the mind to dwell or fantasise on sex. This provides a purity to your exercises and contacts, and gives it your full energy and attention.

Dianism

Intercourse without orgasm to a state of ecstasy.

"Come forth from the stars, and take your fill of love — I am above you and within you. My ecstasy is yours, my joy is to see your joy."

Quodosh (means holy)

The transference and imbibement of sexual secretions, charged to transubstantiate, and thus cause transmutation in the partners. The mingled male and female juices are termed the Elixir. Besides ingestion it can also be used to anoint objects and to charge them

But — call me wimpish if you like — I didn't like all that; and of course just because you can make a glossy website doesn't necessarily mean that in the real world (if there is such a place) you know jack shit about real tantra and real magick. It's not always easy to separate the wheat from the ... well not chaff, exactly, but masturbatory fantasies.

William Gray told me once that there was a surefire rule: If they're after your money then they're a waste of time; if they're not after your money they're probably still a waste of time, but it would do no harm to see what they might offer.

Have a look for others yourself. There's a gentle one by Lady Galadriel of the Grove of the Unicorn, which gives techniques of Western Sex Magick using Arthurian imagery and the Sacred Well, at *ravenfamily.org/ffetch/flowwell/flowing.php*.

Or there's a site called 'The 93 Current' which lists

Thelemic groups and books at *93current.de/groups.shtml*. Many of them seem rather intense, and earnest — not a bad thing! — but personally I don't want groups. And I don't want to agonise at intellectual levels about the true meaning of *Do what thou Wilt.* I think I prefer the calmer, warmer but still challenging words of St. Augustine of Hippo who once wrote: "Ama, et fac quod vis" which can be translated as "Love! And then do what thou Wilt." In other words, every good action is an action according to love.

So would I find within the great beastly realms of cyber-space those techniques which we sought? There's a lot of very dark stuff attached to Thelema to be honest. I quite like some of it, make no mistake, but I didn't really want to delve into Margaret's sexual secretions in an alchemickal sort of way, and I couldn't see her lying there letting me. I didn't want to use robes, organise group rituals or ceremonies, take initiations, visualise my prick as a lance and her cunt as a cauldron, or have to hand over responsibility for progress to anyone else. There wasn't anything I could stumble upon which might be suitable for two lovers who wanted sex, fun and cosmic illumination in roughly that order.

I suppose after having spent very many years having The Hermit from the tarot pack as my Significator, I now wanted to be within the ambience of The Lovers. I wanted human things, and not communion with the dread beings from the dark side of magick — fascinating and seductive though they undoubtedly are.

And I think I realised then that I didn't, after all, want the Magick Button. I didn't really want some cool technique which would trigger everything off without effort. I wanted something mutual, something warm and human and natural rather than inspired by ascetics living in caves in the foothills of the Himalayas or, even colder and bleaker, downtown Los Angeles. I wanted to wear my heart on my sleeve, make a fool of myself perhaps, have more picnics, but then find bliss on all levels between her arms, and within her head and heart. I wanted the warmth, the woolly socks at the end of her long legs, the bright personality, affection and wicked fun. Obviously I was gagging for it by this time.

Alright alright … confession: I who had always revelled in my self-containment, was lonely. I missed her. The magicks we did together up until this point were more like prayers.

On an impulse, perhaps prompted by the Google Angel, I put the words Prayer and Sex into the search box, and to my dismay came up with about 2 billion sites where I could learn "Healing Prayers for Sex Addiction." In the middle of them all, however, was the roughly written but effective Temple of the Goddess website, by the horny looking Anya Deva at *goddessherself.com/tantra.htm* which offered the following:

> Tip: You can consider yourself a true Tantrica if you enjoy these two things a lot: fucking and praying.

Well that sounded good! Just what I wanted. Anya Deva seemed a hopeful sort about such things as love and the Kundalini, all long hair and red lipstick, and she never missed a chance to sell audio CDs, charms and protective talismans, and some top quality Love Magic massage oil. I wasn't gonna buy any of it but we were already true Tantricas according to her. Being a Russian émigré I doubt if she had ever heard of Crowley but then again many in the New Age masses haven't, and if she'd met him in his prime he'd have tried to have her all ends up and make her into his Scarlet Woman (though I think she might have been a match for him). In his and her eyes prayer and sex are inseparable.

So for those souls reading this who still might want to follow the Thelemic Path of Western Tantra, what might they learn from Aleister Crowley? I suppose it is simply the injunction: Dare to be different. And if you want to use the Wiccan wisdom, the third line of which was actually paraphrased from him:

> There is no Grace
> there is no Guilt.

an it harm none
do what thou Wilt...

Or as it might be paraphrased yet further by the horny spirit of the Ashington Lad made manifest in the avatar of Maxwell, the Sun King of Maple Street: *Wrrrrrrrrh … Get stuck in, hinny!*

Oh but I wanted M back. I wanted the sex that was like a prayer: intense and hopeful and aimed toward the highest.

And so I hated Brussels even more, and saw it as the rival. It was keeping her from me. It was as real to me as one of her sloping-browed foreskinless ex-boyfriends. I became dead jealous, juvenile and very petty. Of course I tried to give her some guff about me actually being the Eternal Child rather than simply childish, but I think she saw through it. She had to do a lot of work during our phone calls, reassuring me — not always successfully. Then when all my pouting failed I did my Nostradamus thing and gave her my cosmic vision:

- The entity known as the European Community will collapse
- France and Germany will break away to form an alternative, and invite their sycophants to join
- The émigrés in Brussels will leave on the last gravy train, clinging to it like it was the last helicopter out of Saigon, and go back to their natural homes
- The comet Wormwood will hit Brussels in 2012[12]
- England will never win anything at football until they replace Beckham.

She wasn't impressed. Her work was there, her clients all there. There were things that needed sorting, and we needed luck. No love is ever easy or simple, is it? Raising the Kundalini and becoming a Geordie Sex God was becoming infinitely less important than having her leave Brussels to come and live with

---

12. I made that up.

me. We struck wrong notes on the phone like dial tones, and I figured that if my logick wouldn't work then I had to get back to the magick.

"I've found a brilliant exercise," I told her, determined to keep on track and referring to Anya Deva's site. "We'll do it when you come back. It's a meditation that we can perform together before sex to make it tantric. The perfect union. If anything will awaken serpents mutually this will. We have to remember our quest."

I tried hard to visualise her, putting up the small cinema screen on which all my thoughts project, which is located about 18" before my face, but to the left side. Until I met Margaret I thought everyone had this screen, and saw their thoughts enacted upon it in the same way. When she pointed out that this is quite unusual I suddenly realised why a succession of girlfriends and two wives wondered why I never seemed to be listening to them, simply staring into space, when in fact I was 'seeing' everything they described. And so I was seeing Margaret now, standing next to me, and I missed her dreadfully. Oh god how I hated the phone, and this means of communicating through words alone. And I hated the European Union and had done before she had appeared. There's a moral in that of course, but that's another arcanum and a web-page too far.

"Tell me what we'll do …" she said, excited in that child-like way of hers, creating the future, both of us determined to make it happen.

"We'll sit on the bed facing each other. We'll breathe deeply and slowly. We will put our hands on our own chests and feel our own heartbeats. Then, when we feel connected, we'll touch each other's hearts, and feel the loving beat. At the same time we will look into each other's eyes, look into infinity, without focussing, and we will see each other's ancient soul. Then I'll say something nice and romantic, and then we'll fuck until our fillings ache."

"We did that in St Ives," she pointed out. I could hear her clanking away in Brussels making herself some camomile and apple tea.

"Not quite. We didn't do the heartbeat thingy. And we know a lot more now. This time sex will be a four way orgy: me and you; my anima with your animus.

"Okay," she said, game for anything. "When I get back. Soon. But when I do get back, I've got to unpack first …"

Anya Deva writes in a simple way that I rather like.

> Tantric practices are closely connected with awakening the inner Goddess, or Kundalini energy, who is feminine in her nature. She is the essence of the self, just like the essence of every atom, the inner fire, and aroused by any kind of activity that feels good, therefore, pleases her: dancing or music, but especially, sex. She responds to a playful, non forceful method, and when you make love, connect to your partner's very essence, and play as if you were playing with a kitten. She will trust you and will respond to you. She will hide and withdraw as soon as you will try to control her or control your actions with your mind. She is the consciousness of the body, the dormant of the inner wisdom thousands of years old who is in the same time an ever young and beautiful maiden possessing a tremendous power. She is wisdom of the body and doesn't like to deal with logic of the mind.

She has obviously had some good sex herself because she writes quite rhapsodically about how Tantra's real goal is the union of two free souls, without attachment, bound by a love that equals and is God. To her this love can be compared to nothing on earth because it is truly a divine union which both partners have to be ready for spiritually. It is a union which is above ego, and gives a merge on all levels, resulting in the most beautiful sex.

> Spiritual love is subtle, like the sound of a violin, love by means of the body is like an earthquake, both give different types of orgasm, and combination of both is a complete satisfaction and bliss. And both are the great aid for a good relationship, when sex is also a means of communication between two lovers — communication of deepest togetherness, that brings you physical comfort and peace. Sex is a prayer for body.

God she must have had some fun between the sheets! This seemed a lot healthier and more accessible than the Days and Nights of Thelema. I hope that, for her, it wasn't a one-off with some coke-snorting fly-by-night from east-side New York, muttering about 'connecting' and 'impeccability' and 'having us some down-time, honey.' I hope her shop is successful. I hope she can do love-spells which can charm Margaret from the snares and lairs of Brussels, and I wonder if she will accept my Maestro debit card.

Okay, I promised earlier that I would use Freddie Yam's technique as a very last resort, if all else failed. Remember when he wrote: "Waking the Kundalini is simple. Just move the prana down and the apana up until they meet and combine." I was gonna save that for very last but as I was by myself I had to do it now, when Margaret was over there moving among the upper levels of the Tower of Babel. Then if it succeeded I'd pick her up from Heathrow with the vertical pupils of a serpent, and she'd be dead impressed.

Well, I went to work that day determined to follow Yam's instructions as soon as I got home, though not before I'd hoovered, straightened the furniture, sorted out my nose hair and checked my emails. My two chums at work, Caroline and

Debbie, could see that I was bit pre-occupied.

"'Ere git-face, wot's up with you then?" asked the blonde.

"He hasn't had it for a while, that's wot," said the dark one.

They're respectful like that, see. Well they have to be coz I carry them.

"Lissen girls, I've got a lot on my mind. Tonight I'm gonna move the prana down and the apana up until they meet and combine."

"Eh?" they asked in unison, echoing my old Dad, though neither of them had been anywhere near Ashington. In fact neither of them been further north than the NEC in Birmingham, where they went to throw their steaming knickers at those fat little boys of 'Wham.'

So I explained. "I'm gonna raise the Kundalini. I'm gonna become like unto a God."

"Knobhead" said the dark one.

"Dickhead," said the blonde.

They had adopted strange asanas of their own as they bent double laughing, heads almost touching, holding each other for balance.

"That's classic penis envy you're displaying," said I with massive dignity. I felt sorry for them actually, because one day this posture would cause havoc with their own Kundalinis. Besides, a Serpent King is not without honour save in his own country, as the boy Yeheshua once nearly said.

I was a bit distant for the rest of that day, and in truth I was a bit worried. This concept of 'apana' was completely new to me and a bit troubling. As Yam said, "apana is associated with defecation." I hadn't a clue what he meant. In his own words:

> The sleeping Kundalini is said to coil around the coccyx, the vestigial tailbone that curves downward and inward from the bottom of the spine. The tip of the

coccyx is very close to the anus. Moreover, the bundle of nerves that exits from it, the coccygeal plexus, innervates the skin around the anus. The nearest plexus above it, the sacral plexus, innervates the anal sphincter muscles. One or both of these plexuses are the likeliest anatomical analogues to the first and second chakras of yogic physiology, the muladhara and svadhisthana

Well it made sense to him. After making sure that his spine, when supine, was as straight as possible, he maintained his concentration and stilled his thoughts while he went through various techniques that I'll describe when I try them myself. He found that over the period of several days the sensations he experienced ranged from an increasingly bright and dense light in his head, to the sense of something like a voltage potential building up between his head and the area near his anus, as if a spark were getting ready to jump between them. He also had the intuitive sense that he could help bring about the Kundalini explosion by making deliberate isometric contractions of the muscles of his anus, buttocks, perineum and thighs. He felt that if there was a key to the whole thing, it was splitting his attention so that it focused simultaneously on his anus and the light in his head. This seemed to increase the feeling that a spark was getting ready to jump between them. He focused fiercely and simultaneously on the head and anus, driving the polarization to the breaking point, creating a weird certainty that the explosion was about to occur. To steel his nerves as the brink approached, he fixed part of his attention on the conviction that the event would be benevolent.

Well this was it. My flat was tidy and calm. The carpet was spotless and the hoover neatly stacked away. My nose hairs had never been more fiercely trimmed and the breath could hiss through each nostril without making the sound of Aeolian Harps, while the inbox of Outlook Express was purged of the

93 new offers for viagra, cialis, and painless penis enlargement. This was the moment of my destiny: it needed either a wise fool or a brave coward to light the serpent fires, not just for my sake or Margaret's sake, but for sake of all mankind: it needed an Ashington Lad.

Cometh the hour, cometh the man, as we Tantrikas say.

Lying on the floor of my sitting room I stretched my spine and breathed in a 6-3 rhythm: that is, breathe in for six seconds, hold for three; out for six, hold for three. I stretched my spine and tried to induce a feeling of hollowness in it, while visualising a light in my head.

As I breathed out, I tried to push energy downward, while gently contracting the muscles in my neck and chest. I contracted and relaxed the muscles of my abdomen, inducing a feeling of building up energy. And at the lowest part of my spine I tried to induce the feeling of sending pranic energy up toward my head, helped by gently contracting the muscles around my anal sphincter — more commonly known among the non-yogis as a bum-hole.

There was a gentle surging, a vague fluttering of light and lightness. I think I managed the apana thing — sort of skimming something up and along from the base of spine toward my head. I say 'skimming' because that was the image that came to my mind's eye: like a flat stone across a pond, touching the surface briefly and lightly. I did that several times. But ... but ... nothing happened. I was aware of energies like electrical charges, if that's the right term, at the base of my spine and also the back of my head, but it wasn't powerful. I had no sense that something awesome was about to be unleashed. I tried again.

This time I tried intoning. No, I wasn't gonna go for the OM so beloved of the New Agers, or the AUMGN that Crowley chanted, thinking the sound vibrations were so powerful that any magician using it would be able to control the universal forces. Instead I used the AWEN of Celtic tradition. "The word 'awen' is used by some modern Druids as a Celtic equivalent to the Sanscrit word 'aum,' intoning it when doing trancework, thusly: 'aah-ooo-enn.'" This from *neopagan.net/DruidSymbols.htm*

Now this felt really good: vibrations up and down the body as if I'd put a vibrating object on the crown of my head. But there was no sense of brilliance, no sense of immanence, just a good shaking on the surface levels, a bit like what you can get from the washing machine in its spin cycle.

I tried the techniques again the next day, and once in the middle of the night when I woke unexpectedly.

Nothing. *Rien.* Not even strong dreams.

What worked for Freddie Yam clearly wasn't gonna work for me. Was he lucky? Was I doing it wrong? I think the fact that I was doing it myself was something of a brake. After all, the original idea was to have mutual tantrik sex with Margaret. All of these exercises by myself, while worthy enough, were like trying to achieve a zen-like clapping with one hand. I'd try the same thing but with her next to me, touching my heart, giving me her love.

The phone rang. I saw the Belgian number and my heart leapt.

"I'll see you tonight," she said. Her voice was soft, and made me softer.

Now where was that hoover, the teddy hot-water bottle and the vanilla bean room spray?

Chapter 9

What I was searching for ... cannot in fact be given by another person, cannot be found in a theory, or a profession, no matter how well-meaning. It is only, I am convinced, to be had, or not had, through living. There are no experts in loving, no scholars of living, no doctors of the human emotions and no gurus of the soul. But we need not be alone; friendship is a precious gift, and all that we need to do to see is remove the blinders

jeffreymasson.com/

When I was a young man, me and Maxwell hitchhiked around the country. We started from Ashington, more or less circumnavigated England in a deosil direction, and arrived back at the Tyne Bridge after what seemed like years. We must have stank. I carried our tent, ground sheet, sleeping bags, cooking equipment (including pan, kettle, gas stove), cutlery, can opener, torch, bog roll, maps and food; he carried his banjo, on which he could play only three chords but very fast. At one point we found ourselves in Weston Super Mare, meeting up with another Ashington friend of ours called Apollo Fuge, and while we sat drinking in the windy bar at the end of the now defunct Birnbeck Pier, with the noises of the sea beneath and the gulls above, I had another of my *Little Moments*, as I tended to think of these possessions: another 'Stopping the World.' Many years later, researching Dion Fortune, I would stand on this same spot and remember that time with my pals, and summon up the mood, the stillness, the descent of wise grace and the not-quite-thereness.

I can sense it again now as I reminisce, and see it on my cinema screen with detail and intensity. At the back of my mind I also have an image, explanatory perhaps, of the serpents crossing on the caduceus, which equates with the channels of the ida and pingala looping back and forth across the sushumna. So as the other two quaffed their weak southern beer and their chairs scraped on the bare floorboards above the rising tide, and Maxwell regaled us with his tales of Honolulu Foot-Fighting, at which he was — he assured us — renowned as something of an adept in the back lanes of Ashington, and as the Something descended for those seconds going on for infinity, was it actually my future selves that took over my head?

"But Maxy man," asked Fuge, somewhat churlishly but not unreasonably, "where *exactly* in Ashington did ye lorn Honolulu Foot-Fightin'?"

Maxwell leaned forward conspiratorially, smiling mysteriously, brushing his shoulder-length blonde hair away from his evilly-handsome, fight-battered face, and I came back into the world instantly coz — cosmic consciousness or not — I just had to hear this one!

"Lissen bonny lad," he said in a low voice, looking around him, "Ye'd nivver believe iz if Aah telt ye …"

Well I was nice to them for the rest of the afternoon, and let them beat me at table football. Then Maxwell kindly allowed me to be his coolie again as I hefted the gear down the edge of the dusty dual carriageway while he walked ahead singing Geordie pit songs at the top of his voice with his banjo on his back. And as I look back today, staring into the depths of the monitor, like a crystal ball accessing the Akashic records, I discovered that Google couldn't find doodly-squat about Honolulu foot-fighting, so I'm beginning to lose faith in them.

In the last chapter Mystress Angelique Serpent wrote about tracking back through the DNA and becoming, or rather experiencing, her own grandfather, and she linked this with the Kundalini experience. It made me think of the time when I had had a startling experience with my second daughter Kirsty, as I walked her to infants' school one morning.

Y'see being a Dad was always something of a revelation to me, and a bewilderment. I never felt Dad-like in age; I never felt that I had the substance that Dads should have. I always found it astonishing that me, little me, should have these tiny gorgeous beings following me about and sometimes looking at me as if I were a minor God.

I knew that Kirsty was troubled, although she was an uncomplaining little girl. And I suddenly realised why: there was a school trip, and we had forgotten to give her some money to spend. As I reached into my pocket and bent down to hand over a pound it suddenly happened. I became my Dad giving me pocket money; then his dad giving him some pennies, and my great grandfather doing likewise to my grandfather, and it was like Russian dolls popping out of each other, the smallest being tucked away in the farthest history of my DNA. It was like an Apostolic succession: I had a sense of this lineage of dads giving to their children — whether it was pocket money, prezzies or food — and passing on their *dadness*.

Well I'm not quite sure of the relevance of this, except that other acknowledged or self-professed tantrikas have experienced similar, so maybe I'm just staking a claim, or explaining to the grown-up Kirsty why her Old Dad may have seemed to drift off at times.

And maybe it's all to do with prana, as most yogis insist. After all prana is everywhere, prana is Shakti, Shakti is Kundalini, Kundalini is (apparently) linked with DNA, with ancestors and guides, past/present/future are all one, and everything flows into all.

We are one another. And given just the slightest unusual effort in expressing love, then we are all tantrikas in one way or another.

It was late, 1 am. I waited on the platform at Chippenham Station. Margaret was coming back from Brussels for 36 hours with me. She would be exhausted and jet-lagged after three weeks of international flights and furiously demanding work to earn a crust and create a future. I had in my car, the plug-in electric blanket, a Tescos chicken salad, flowers, some charming and prepared banter, huge excitement and a lot of anxiety. Courtship over distance is not easy when communication is almost exclusively by phone, which is a medium I find difficult. Tensions and misunderstandings had arisen; we squabbled; I had been childish; it had seemed at times that our worlds might be too far apart for the light and love to traverse the bleakness of interstellar space and our own fears.

It's funny, a mage can turn inward and find whole universes and strange dimensions to explore within, yet a few hundred earth-miles can become an uncrossable void, and cause our voices to sound very thin and cold as they sought to travel over its depths and our own darkness. The train came and roared off.

"Hello," she said, when we found ourselves alone on the cold platform at one thirty in the morning, her in her business suit and surrounded by a small fortress of suitcases, dark-haired and gorgeous as ever, moving her weight from foot to foot as I approached.

I stood there trying to find some persona that would be mid-way between that of the great and protective du Lac, ready to storm battlements and rescue his queen, and his gently-fussy attentive squire, wanting to carry her cases, unpack them, and tuck her up in bed with thick socks and hot drink.

"So you've come all this way just to see me ..." I countered, and in a quiet way, in the cold and night, all the anxieties dissolved at once and I realised then that raising the Kundalini, which I had always imagined to the *ne plus ultra* of human achievement, must necessarily be far easier and far less important than effective human loving.

"You haven't got serpent eyes yet," she said, looking into mine and making me melt.

"Come home …"

On a whim I typed "Lancelot and Tantra" into Google and got straight through to School of Tantra at *schooloftantra.com/articles/* where they had a piece about Polyamory, illustrated by a painting of *Lancelot & Guinevere* by Eleanor Fortescue-Brickdale, which was the hook. The aim of this organisation was to: "Investigate the possibilities of a polyamorous (more than one love) lifestyle. Ask us how you can make more love in your life, relate from your highest self with your lovers and housemates, uplevel jealousy into compersion (joy at your lovers' joy), and give them each the attention, companionship, touch and sexual-loving they need." Their rates were quite steep, their classes all on Hawaii, yet their takers seemed many.

"Don't even think about it," came a uni-amorous voice from behind me, so I made apologies to the pixels and moved quickly on. Well I had to, coz we were off on another adventure.

With Margaret's presence I tried the Freddie Yam technique again, combining it with the touching the heart and finding the pulse thing mentioned earlier. Listen, it felt good, and there was a kind of trembling of light within, and those luminous flickerings at the base of my spine, but there was no sense that it might suddenly explode and surge. Was I distracted by having my Shakti's hand on my heart? By her warmth? I tried it again but there was nothing immanent, just a clear memory of that time on the couch, in Ashington, when, as far as I can understand it, the Kundalini had coursed up and down my body and soul and a presence appeared next to me that I likened to Jesus. Then I opened my eyes. It was suddenly clear to me who or what that Jesus figure had really been:

Me. Dark haired and bearded, benign and loving toward that strange young boy. Smiling humorously, with absolute affection. It had to be me. I was linking back with myself, haunting myself as I had done in other circumstances.

"Are you alright?" asked Margaret, seeing my face

change as my brain cells started working. "Did you raise the Kundalini?"

I took a deep breath.

"Not now. Not tonight. But I'm pretty sure I did many years ago on another planet, in a faraway place called Ashington."

"That's nice darling," she answered, smiling sweetly. "Shall we have some biscuits?"

I realised it was all linked together: dreams, synchronicity, spirit guides, Dion Fortune, spirit of place, DNA, Ashington and Shamballah, gurus and pitmen, Crowley and Maxwell, alchemy and fatherhood, daughters and deities and doing what thou Wilt. It was perhaps best symbolised as the Worm Ouroboros expressing the concept 'All Is One,' which was neatly defined as:

> Ouroboros is an ancient alchemy symbol depicting a snake or dragon [DNA] swallowing its own tail, constantly creating itself and forming a circle. It is the Wheel of Time – The Alchemy Wheel – 12 Around 1 – to manifest grid programs that give the illusion of linear time allowing souls to experience emotions.
>
> *crystalinks.com/ouroboros.html*

Now the Great Winged Serpent aka The Worm Ouroboros, is not generally seen a lot in Ashington these days since cable telly arrived, but it links me by showing me that Past/Present/Future are One. I'm an ageing tantrika, I'm a young Ashington Lad; there is no difference. It is that energy which twists and turns and slides through life, that we can sense in moments of grand passion (always beautiful and always painful), or that helps us grow wings to escape the gravities of despair. It enables us to rear and hiss, with optional poison, and also shed skins to renew ourselves. It is the twin snakes on the caduceus, recrossing the central themes of love's spark, love's flame, love's ember and dust, always at a differing level, sometimes leading up to the soaring heights of wisdom when you can, briefly, fly as dragons can fly: through, under and over the earth which spawned you.

Maybe we don't need specious techniques. Just as placebos can have bewildering powers to heal, even when the subjects actually know that they're placebos and not the 'real' thing, I'm sure now it doesn't matter what you do in these spiritual activities or how you do it, as long as the intent is there. In fact, right from the start, one of the most effective things I adopted in this odd business of magick was that which I mentioned earlier: learning to regard everything that happened, every event, accident and incident, as a secret dealing between myself, and the innermost spirit of my Gods.

Of course I made a right prick of myself at first, but with a bit of discrimination it helped things take off. Although I don't think much in terms of Gods now the essence of that approach is still valid. As a boy it turned Ashington into Shamballah, Tir N'an Og, Narnia, Perelandra, Utopia and, often, Mordor; the old colliers, hard as fuck and wise as bodhisattvas, were my first gurus, and I venerated them; Mam became my Dark Goddess and Dad my Sacrificed God and they took my adoration; every girlfriend was an initiatrix, nymph, witch queen or dakini, with awesome powers of spellcraft; every enemy was a Dweller on the Threshold who had to be dealt with; and my children were all expressions of the alchemical Great Work, which transforms lead into pure and priceless gold. I'm not sure what Ron the Neck was, but there's nothing there a good Banishing Ritual wouldn't fix, or failing that, a long weekend of colonic irrigation.

Did I need to go surfing cyberspace when the magickal landscapes were always within me? Did I need to find and raise the Kundalini at all when all things flow into the One?

Maybe those people who experienced the Kundalini as an express train thundering through their consciousness or as an atom bomb going off, felt this because until then they had lived steady lives, safe lives and dead lives like bottles on a shelf: when they were shaken the energies were always going to explode. So maybe if we live active lives, with all the torments, shocks, and agitated delights of everyday existence, the Kundalini is released in a steady stream without us realising. Love, and then do what you will. Live, and then love how you can.

And after all — c'mon folks — surely there are better ways to spend a Saturday night than thrusting 10,000 times, clenching your rectal muscles, raising apana, breathing through alternate nostrils, collecting juices, adopting bizarre postures and all with the knowledge that Monday's dread grind is fast approaching. Surely there is a life to be lived before the Grim Reaper (whom I always visualised as Maxwell in a duffel coat) comes laughing toward us? I'm certain now that it doesn't matter what you do as long as you do something.

Margaret leaned against me as we sat up in bed. Sophisticated continental that she is, she wore the old shirt in the faded colours of my beloved but infuriating Newcastle United, thick grey socks and cuddled the teddy hot-water bottle. Over the months we had almost swapped roles, so that where she was smart I was thick, and my cleverness fitted into her dopiness quite neatly, like the tails and heads of the yin and yang. Now she was absorbed in the gossip of Chat magazine while I browsed a dead hard book about the iniquities of psychoanalysis. As she lay against me, her lips moving as she read, I felt a kind of bliss, the true satori of a man who has been healed. Did I really want the classic Kundalini experience, all bells and flashing lights and claxons?

And how did the ecstasy of my quiet Kundalini experience in Ashington compare with my other non-Kundalini highs? That's easy to answer. Don't need any navel gazing for this.

Nothing, absolutely nothing, could compare with holding my children in my arms and feeling a surge of unselfish, pure and unconditional love that I knew would last for the rest of my life, and make me determined to be the best dad, dream the best dreams, have the best visions, show the awesome dad powers as best I could, for their sake. Nothing could compare with the first moments of falling and flailing in love with Margaret, the folly, the silliness, the beyond-time heart-thumping, the stopping of the world and the sharp gasp when *She* steps off the train. All the tantrikas in the world, whether in their caves or ashrams, could not have better connectedness and expansion than I had then, with my children in the next room and Margaret's weight against mine, her warmth making me whole again.

We have probably all released Kundalini energies, goddess energies, one way or another. Forget the chakra crap, forget the pranayama, the channels, the postures, the poses and the marmas. To be fair it's not entirely bollocks, and we tried a lot of things too personal to mention here, but you can act *as if* it is and not lose a whole lot. As Arthur Koestler said in his last days, there are only two important things to life:

> 1. We must be connected to something, whether it's a person, place, object or idea.

> 2. It's more important to love than be loved.

And that, surely, is all we need to be going on with. As the Ouroboros/Dragon/Serpent King/Kundalini teaches, we are all parts of one whole, we link with one another. A line from D.H. Lawrence's *Apocalypse* sprang to my mind: "that I am part of the earth ..." I Googled for the very last time and within a second found the quote I wanted.

For man, the vast marvel is to be alive. For
man, as for flower and beast and bird, the
supreme triumph is to be most vividly, most
perfectly alive. Whatever the unborn and
the dead may know, they cannot know the
beauty, the marvel of being alive in the flesh.
The dead may look after the afterwards. But
the magnificent here and now of life in the
flesh is ours, and ours alone, and ours only
for a time.

Doesn't that make your heart sing? These were the
last words he wrote, remember. I had printed them out and
read them out to Margaret but she was too busy reading about
lipstick, the Beckhams and face cleansers to take them on board
properly. And there's more ...

We ought to dance with rapture that we
should be alive and in the flesh, and part of
the living, incarnate cosmos. I am part of
the sun as my eye is part of me. That I am
part of the earth my feet know perfectly,
and my blood is part of the sea. My soul
knows that I am part of the human race, my
soul is an organic part of the great human
soul, as my spirit is part of my nation. In
my own very self, I am part of my family.
There is nothing of me that is alone and
absolute except my mind, and we shall find
that the mind has no existence by itself, it
is only the glitter of the sun on the surface
of the waters.

en.wikiquote.org/wiki/D._H._Lawrence

Could we want better? Could we want healthier?
Close your books, switch off your computers, say bye-bye to
Googling. If anyone loves you, love them back. If no-one loves

you, give love to yourself, and then gently offer some simple loving-kindness to anyone who comes along in future, whether you think they deserve it or not.

Something like that, anyway.

In a manful and almost contemptuous way I threw the teddy to one side and pulled Margaret toward me. She was no longer a Shakti but a warm, luminous, bendy and very human being, flawed and delightful and real, getting old as I grew old, laughing at the things that made me laugh, teasing me rotten. I was not a Serpent King with chakras a-fire but a lovesick Alan, flawed, bewildered and often battered, but ever hopeful.

"I've failed you haven't I? I haven't managed to give you the Serpent Powers, and I'm still struggling with the verb Etre, which is something to do with Being."

She took off her glasses to look at me. She peered into my eyes for the vertical pupils of serpents, shook her head, put her hand on my heart and said in a voice like the warm honey of the elixir of life:

"Come here …"

Postscript

Some of the URLs given in the preceding text may no longer exist, like places in your childhood that you can never revisit. This doesn't matter. The whole point of the book is that you grab your mouse and go looking for whatever it is you might need, tracking down that which is fresh and relevant now, trusting the Web Angel to bring you to life and to light and to love – with a bit of learning thrown in.

Margaret and I are married now.

She lives with me full time, but still doesn't know where the hoover is.

Next year, as part of a difficult but not impossible challenge, she will teach me to swim, and wield a golf bat.

And I still loathe Brussels.

www.ingramcontent.com/pod-product-compliance
Lightning Source LLC
Chambersburg PA
CBHW030933090426
42737CB00007B/415